Global English

취업성공을 위한 글로벌 영어

TOEIC과
영어 취업인터뷰 활용 극대화

백선숙
강희준

SEROMI

Prologue

한국에서 영어 실력은 성공에 언제나 중요한 요소입니다. 많은 성인들이 졸업과 취업, 이직 등의 인생의 크고 작은 성공을 위해 영어를 공부하고 있습니다. 다양한 영어 교육 프로그램으로 선택의 폭이 넓어졌지만, 마치 홍수에 먹을 물이 없는 것처럼 속 시원한 대안은 찾지 못하고 한계를 체험하곤 합니다.

그 이유 중 첫 번째로는 실력을 쌓기 위한 '인내의 시간'을 견디지 못하고 사상누각과 같은 빠른 성취를 이루고자 하는 조급함 때문입니다. 우리가 영어 스피킹을 학습하면서 피하고 싶고 귀찮아 하는 것은 바로 '입을 통한 훈련의 실천'입니다. 머리로 이해했다고 끝나는 게 아니라 꾸준한 연습이 꼭 필요하다는 것을 잘 알면서도 미적거리게 됩니다. 꾸준한 노력과 인내의 연습시간이 필요하기 때문에 쉽사리 손에 넣고 만족하기 힘든 것입니다. '천재는 1%의 영감과 99%의 땀으로 이루어진다."는 에디슨의 명언의 원래 의도는 애초에 1%의 영감이 없다면 나머지 99%의 노력은 물거품이라는 뜻이었다고 합니다. 99%의 노력과 인내를 가능하게 하는 1%의 원동력은 바로 '영어로 이루고자 하는 여러분의 꿈'입니다. 영어공부에 지칠 때마다 열정의 불을 다시 지필 수 있는 자신의 꿈을 다시 떠올려 보는 것이 영어실력 향상에 핵심이 될 수 있을 것입니다.

학생들이 영어학습에 한계를 느끼는 두 번째 이유로는 다양한 분야의 영어공부를 해야 한다는 부담감에 '번아웃 증후군'에 쉽게 빠지기 때문입니다. 대학에서 TOEIC, 회화, 에세이 작성, TOEIC SPEAKING, 영어 인터뷰, 전공실용영어 등 다양한 영어 관련 과목을 학생들을 위해 개설하여 운영하고 있습니다. 누구나 학기

초에는 열심히 해서 영어실력을 증진하겠다는 다짐을 하지만, 몇 주 지나지 않아 초심을 잃어가는게 대부분의 모습입니다. 이를 지켜보며 가장 안타까운 점은 학생들이 영어학습을 흥미로운 언어스킬을 배워가는 과정이라고 여기지 않고, 높은 학점/말하기 점수/회화실력/공인성적 등을 위한 각기 다른 분야의 학문을 따로 공부해야만 하는 것으로 여겨 많은 스트레스를 받고 있다는 것입니다.

이에 필자는 이 책을 통해 영어 학습 본연의 흥미를 줄 뿐만 아니라, 동시에 여러분의 크고 작은 실질적인 목표달성을 도울 수 있도록 구성하였습니다. 각 Unit은 생활에서 쉽게 접할 수 있는 주제로 선정하였고, Unit에서 목표하는 Grammar를 활용하여 스피킹과 쓰기연습을 할 수 있는 충분한 기회를 제공하도록 구성하였습니다. 여기까지는 대부분의 영어회화 교재 구성과 비슷할 수 있지만, 이 책의 특징이자 타 교재들과의 도드라진 차이점은 각 Unit에서 학습한 내용을 TOEIC과 영어 취업인터뷰에 바로 적용하여 영어학습의 효율성을 극대화하여 구성하였다는 점입니다. 아무쪼록 많은 이들에게 이 책이 유익하게 작용하여 유창한 영어 구사 능력을 갖는 동시에 취업 성공까지 이루길 바랍니다.

영어는 비즈니스의 크고 작은 성공에 큰 발판이 되어주는 도구가 될 뿐만 아니라, 생각과 경험의 폭을 넓혀주는 소중한 여러분의 자산이 될 것이라 믿습니다. 멋진 꿈을 위해 노력하는 여러분을 응원하겠습니다.

2023년 02월

Contents

Global English

UNIT 01

Greeting and Salutations

• UNIT GOALS

- Use formal greeting
- Introduce yourself to the group

• GRAMMAR FOCUS

- Yes/No Questions
- Wh-Questions

• JOB SUCCESS

- TOEIC : 문장의 구성요소(Components of a sentence)

01 Introduction

Should e-mails open with Dear, Hi or Hey?

It's time people stopped using the word 'Dear…' to start work e-mails. That's according to Giselle Barry, a woman who works in the United States Congress. Ms. Barry thinks 'Dear' is too **intimate** and makes it sound like you have a personal relationship with the person you are writing to.
It seems she's not alone. E-mail and the internet have changed the rules about how to write. In the past, there was no choice, but now you can see e-mails from people starting with 'hello,' 'hi' and even 'hey.'
But not everyone is as relaxed about this as Ms. Barry. **Etiquette** expert Jean Broke-Smith says, 'I'm **fed up with** people writing 'Hi Jean' when they've never met me.'
'If you're sending a business e-mail you should begin 'Dear…' - like a letter. You are presenting yourself. **Politeness** and etiquette are essential.

(Note: this article is based on an original story written by James Morgan from BBC News.)

02 Warm Up Activity

A. Did you understand the words in **bold**? Choose the correct meaning.

❶ **Intimate**
1. A word for people you don't know very well
2. word for people you have a private relationship with

❷ **Etiquette**
1. Another word that means writing
2. The rules of correct behavior in certain situations

❸ **Fed up**
1. Bored or annoyed
2. Not hungry any more

❹ **Politeness**
1. A noun meaning the right way to speak and act without upsetting people
2. A noun meaning dressing well

B. Distinguish formal expression from informal one.

1. What's going on? / How are you doing? / What's up? (Formal, Informal)
2. How are you? / How do you do? (Formal, Informal)
3. Hello / Hi / Hey (Formal, Informal)
4. Good morning? / Good afternoon? / Good evening? (Formal, Informal)
5. How's everything? / Long-time no see. / It's been a while (Formal, Informal)
6. How have you been? (Formal, Informal)
7. Good to see you. / Nice to see you. (Formal, Informal)
8. It's nice to meet you. / Pleased to meet you. (Formal, Informal)

C. **Discussion 1.** Do you think that the internet has made the language you use less formal? Is that a good or a bad thing? How important is it to be polite?

Discussion 2. Do you think that Cabin Crew should use formal language? If so, why? or Why not?

➡

03 Conversation

VARIOUS GREETINGS

A. Formal greeting

- Teacher Paul, I'd like to introduce you to my friend Linda. Linda, this is teacher Paul.
- How do you do, Linda? Pleased to meet you.
- How do you do? My pleasure meeting you, teacher Paul.

B. Introducing others

A Good morning, Fiona. How have you been?

B I'm great. Thank you. Spencer, this is my colleague Kaden. We started working here at the same time, but he's senior to me in the company. He used to work at the Jeju branch before he came to Seoul.

A Hello, Kaden, You can call me Spencer.

C Hello, Spencer. It's nice to meet you.

A It's good to meet you too. I'm all out of business cards. Would it be okay if I give one to you the next time we meet?

C Sure. Here's my business card.

A Thank you.

C. Welcoming visitors

A Mr. Richardson? My name is Carol, Carol Green. We've spoken on the phone before.

B Yes, Ms. Green. How are you?

A Good. It's so nice to finally meet you. So, how was your journey to Korea?

B It wasn't too bad. It was a very long flight though.

A Yes, it will take a while before you get used to the time difference. Well, I'll give you a ride to the hotel. Let me take one of your bags.

B Thank you. Is the hotel close to the conference hall?

A Yes, it is. So it should be convenient enough for you.

B That sound great.

D. Greeting passengers at the check-in counter

Ground Staff Good morning, sir. May I see your ticket and passport?

Passenger Here you are.

Ground Staff All right. How many baggage would you like to check?

Passenger Just one.

E. Greeting passengers at the boarding gate

Cabin Crew	Good afternoon, sir. Welcome aboard. May I see your boarding pass, please?
Passenger	Here it is.
Cabin Crew	Thank you. Please take the aisle to your left.
Passenger	Thanks.
Cabin Crew	You're welcome. Have a nice flight.

PAIR ACTIVITY

Practice each conversation again. You can use your own stories or different ideas.

04 Basic Grammar

Let's learn about *wh-question* words.

What / Who / Where / When / Why

A	**What** do you do for fun?	B	I play basketball.
A	**Who** do you play basketball with?	B	I play basketball with my friends.
A	**Where** do you play?	B	We play at the park.
A	**When** do you play?	B	We play every weekend.
A	**Why** don't you play during the week?	B	Because we are really busy during the week.

Comprehension Check Exercise

Complete the questions with the correct wh-question words.

A ___*What*___ do you do?

B I'm a professor.

A ______________ are your job responsibilities?

B I prepare lessons, mark exams, and teach.

A ______________ do you work?

B I work at a university.

A ______________ do you work there?

B I enjoy working there, so that's why I do it.

A ______________ do you work?

B I only teach on Mondays, Wednesdays, and Fridays.

A ______________ do you work with?

B I work with two other colleagues.

05 Reading

Topic : Likes and Dislikes

When introducing someone, we can talk about the person's like and dislikes. By discussing the person's favorite and least favorite activities, we can get to know the person on a deeper level. We should include when, where, why, and with whom they enjoy doing their favorite activities.

Special Reading

Read about the following people's likes and dislikes and complete the mind maps with information. You don't need to use complete sentences in the bubbles.

I am Kevin, and I like playing games. Actually, I don't like sports at all. I like games that challenge my mind. On weekends, I usually go to Central Park and play chess. Chess teaches you about strategy, and I find that very interesting. I really dislike watching television. I think it is a waste of time. I don't like listening to music either. I'd much rather listen to a lecture from a rally intelligent professor.

I am Anne, and I really love to go shopping. My friends say I'm a shopaholic. I go shopping two or three times a week. On weekends, I might visit nine or ten stores in one day. None of my friends can keep up with me. I really hate working at my current part-time job. I'm a sales clerk in a convenience store. It's not very exciting. I love the job something more active, but I need the job so I can go shopping on the weekends!

Likes :

Anne

Dislikes :

PAIR ACTIVITY

Step 1. Write about your own likes and dislikes.

- My Likes :
- My Dislikes :

Step 2. Ask your partner what he or she thinks about your items. Then fill in the chart.

	Likes	Dislikes
My Partner's name :	▪ ▪	▪ ▪

A I like playing basketball. **What** do you think about it?

B I love it, too. I play basketball quiet often.

A Really? **How often** do you play basketball?

B I play it every Saturday.

A I don't like reading books. **How** about you?

B I don't like reading, either. I'd rather watch TV.

Step 3. Now with the chart above, introduce your partner to the class.

Hello. Let me introduce my partner. Her name is ______________________ .

➡ --

It was great time to talk to her.

06 Grammar Focus

Let's learn about Yes/No questions & *wh-questions.*

In English, there are two basic types of question.

Meaning	1. **Yes/no questions** often begin with the verb **to be**, but can also begin with other **auxiliary verbs**, such as **do**. We ask these when we want a **yes** or **no** answer. **Dave** **Are** you hungry? **Mike** 네, 배고프네요. ➡ **Sarah** **Did** you get here on time? **Emily** 아니요, 버스를 놓쳤어요. ➡ 2. **Wh-questions** start with a question word, such as **who**, **what**, **where**, **when**, **why** or **how**. We ask this type of question when we want **different kinds of information**. These questions cannot be answered with a yes or no. **Dave** **Why** are you so hungry? **Mike** 아침을 못 먹어서요. ➡ **Sarah** **When** did you get here? **Emily** 약 30분 전에요. ➡
Form	1. **Yes/no questions** that begin with the verb **to be** are made with **to be + subject**. **You are** playing football tomorrow. ➡ **The weather was** nice yesterday. ➡ If we start with an **auxiliary verb**, the order is **auxiliary + subject + main verb**. **Jenny can speak** Chinese. ➡ **You went** to the cinema on Saturday. ➡

2. **Wh-questions** can be used to ask about the **subject** or **object** of the verb. Compare these questions:

Who loves Lucy?

Who does Lucy love?

For **subject** questions, the order is **question word + verb + object**.

Mandy wants ice cream for dessert. ➞

Su-ji broke the mirror in the dining room. ➞

Kim answered the phone. ➞

The **object** question form is **question word + auxiliary + subject + verb**.

You **went to the cinema** at the weekend. ➞

Your brother works **at starbucks café**. ➞

You will ask **Mandy** for help. ➞

Take Note

Asking questions with 'how'

The question word how is usually combined with other words when asking for information, such as size, someone's age, or the price of something.

- How ( ) is your apartment?
- How ( ) are your children now?
- How ( ) is the black dress in the window?

Spoken English

A. In formal situations, it is common to respond to a yes/no question by repeating the auxiliary in a complete sentence.

Max　Can you use a computer?
Jill　Yes, I can.

B. In casual spoken English, we do not need to repeat the auxiliary. Answers do not always contain 'yes' or 'no'.

Peter　Do you know the way to the train station?
William　Not really.

Lucy　Shall we order sushi?
Sally　Absolutely!

Comprehension Check Exercise

Rearrange the words to make 'yes/no' and wh-questions.

1. anywhere did you weekend interesting last go?
2. grow up did you where?
3. did for your car new much how pay you?
4. into your when you did move new house?
5. listening to what you are?
6. the game basketball who won?
7. I borrow can your phone?
8. you do watch want movie a tonight to?

07 Activity

Get to know the neighbours

A. Work with a partner. Look at the different doors. Which house would you most/least like to live in? Why? Think about it.

B. With your partner, choose one of the houses and answer the questions. Use your imagination.

- Where is the house? Which country? in a city, a town or a village?
- How big is the house? How many rooms does it have? Does it have a garden?
- Who lives in the house? A family, a couple, a young person, an old person?

C-a. Match the adjectives with the meanings.

confident	funny	generous	kind	reliable
serious	shy	sociable	friendly	humorous

1. is nervous or embarrassed about talking to other people.
2. is careful, sensible and not silly.
3. enjoys spending time with other people.
4. cares about other people.
5. feels sure about their ability to do things.
6. likes to give people things.
7. is good at making you laugh.
8. can be trusted to do something well.

C-b. Choose adjectives you would use to describe a) yourself, b) members of your family. And complete the table with other detail information.

- yourself :
- members of your family :

	Name	Relation	Age	Job/school	Personality
1					
2					
3					
4					

D. Which of these questions do you think are OK to ask someone you don't know very well?

1. What do you do for a living? (A polite way of saying 'what is your job?')
2. How much do you earn?
3. How old are you?
4. Do you have any children?
5. Have you lived/worked here long?
6. Do you have any hobbies?
7. What are your politics?
8. Are you going on holiday this year?

E. Imagine that you are one of the people who lives in the house you chose. You are going to go to a small party for the neighbours. Try to talk to at least 4 of your neighbours and find out some information about them. Don't ask questions which are too personal.

1st Neighbour's name & Characteristic :

➡

2nd Neighbour's name & Characteristic

➡

3rd Neighbour's name & Characteristic

➡

4th Neighbour's name & Characteristic

➡

F. Who was the most interesting person you met? Tell your partner, or the class, and explain why.

➡

08 TOEIC 문장의 구성요소

문장의 구성요소는 무엇이 있나요?

A. 주어

- 역할
- 문장에서의 위치

명사(구)	그 남자는 월요일마다 커피숍을 간다. ________ ________ goes to coffee shop on Mondays.
대명사	그들은 복사기를 구매했다. ________ bought the copy machine.
동명사(구)	그것을 써보는 것이 권장된다. ________ ________ is recommended.

B. 동사

- 역할
- 문장에서의 위치

be동사	그는 그 회사의 대표 이사이다. He ________ the CEO of the company.
일반동사	맨디는 매달 집에 간다. Mandy ________ home every month.
조동사 + 동사원형	우리는 매일 새로운 계획을 할 것이다. We ________ ________ a new plan everyday.

C. 목적어

- 역할
- 문장에서의 위치

명사(구)	1. [타동사+목적어] 맨디는 편지를 받았다. Mandy received ______________ . 2. [전치사+목적어] 고객들은 그 회사의 답변에 만족해 한다. Customers are satisfied with ______________ of the company.
대명사	기술지원팀이 우리를 도와줄 것이다. The technology support team will help ______________ .
to 부정사(구)	우리는 다시 영어공부 하기를 원한다. We want ______________ study English again.
동명사(구)	나는 영화 보는 것을 즐긴다. I enjoy watch ______________ movies. 헨리는 비용을 줄이는 것에 관해 도움이 되는 조언을 찾고 있다. Henry is seeking helpful advice on reducing costs.

D. 보어

❶ 주격 보어

- 주격 보어란?
- 문장에서의 위치

명사	그녀는 상담 전문가이다. She is ____________________________ .
형용사	그녀는 친절하다. She is ____________________________ .

❷ 목적격 보어

- 목적격 보어란?
- 문장에서의 위치

명사	반 학생 모두는 보나를 캡틴으로 선출했다. All classmates elected Bona ______________ .
형용사	모두는 그녀가 총명하다고 생각한다. Everyone considers her ______________ .

01. _______ for recruitment are due on March 25.

(a) Apply (b) Applications

02. They must _______ the employment contract by Friday.

(a) signs (b) sign

03. The latest phone by Samgung _____ less connecting noise than expected.

(a) produces (b) produce

04. Our team manager, Mr. Kim avoids _______ part-timers with complicated tasks.

(a) providing (b) provide

05. The return policy is _______ for new customers to follow.

(a) difficulty (b) difficult

UNIT 02

What's she like?

UNIT GOALS

- Describing a person's appearance and personality

GRAMMAR FOCUS

- Modifiers with present participles and prepositions
- be like, look like

JOB SUCCESS

- TOEIC : RC - 문장의 5문형
- Job Interview : Personality

01 Introduction

My Best Friend

Sol is my best friend. She is very cheerful and friendly. Moreover, she is so warm-hearted that she does not pass by difficulties around her. I once had a hard time catching up with the school schedule. She is the one who helped me by sharing her daily study plan. I was so touched. If there were not such a good friend Sol, I would not finish the course at school successfully.

She likes to try out famous restaurants and have tasty dishes with me. While enjoying food, as most girlfriends do, we love talking about our routines and taking pictures of the food. She also uploads photos and posts reviews on her SNS. It is great fun to explore new restaurants and share tasty meals with her.

Q1. What is Sol like? ➡ ______________________

Q2. What does Sol like? ➡ ______________________

Exercise

Question	Answer
➡	James likes playing football.
What's your house like?	➡
What was your weekend like?	It was very busy. I spent the whole weekend tidying my flat.
What's your dad like?	➡

02 Conversation

CONVERSATION

Which one is she?

A Hello, Kara! Good to see you! Why didn't you come to the meeting yesterday?

B Oh, I wanted to. But I couldn't make it. I went to a concert with Sol.

A Oh! Your best friend, Sol?

B Yes, Here is a photo that I took with her a long time ago. Sol came here on vacation. So, I took her to the concert of her favorite musician. It was an incomparable show and I still believe no one is even close. Now I became a big fan of hers.

A Really? That sounds great! And which one is she? **What does she look like**?

B She is quite tall, with brown hair.

A Wow! Look at you~! You used to have long hair. And **how long is her hair**?

B It's pretty long tousled hair.

A Is she the woman **wearing** the glasses in front of her friends?

B Yes, she is the one **in** a pink hoodie.

PAIR ACTIVITY

Practice each conversation again. You can use your own stories or different ideas.

03 Basic Grammar

Let's learn about 'be like' and 'look like'.

be like and look like	
What's she like?	She's smart, funny, and confident.
What does she look like?	She's tall and good-looking. She has long, curly red hair.
Who does she look like?	She looks like Julia Robers.

성격을 나타내는 단어 (장점)

- prudent 신중한
- sincere 성실한, 진실한
- responsible 책임감 강한
- open-minded 개방적인
- cheerful 활기찬, 발랄한
- understanding 이해심이 많은
- generous 관대한 후한
- confident 자신감 있는
- sociable 사교적인
- polite 예의 바른
- flexible 융통성이 있는
- caring 상냥한, 잘 돌봐주는
- outgoing, active 외향적인, 적극적인
- energetic 열정, 정열적인
- organized 체계적인, 정리 잘하는
- trustworthy, reliable 신뢰할 수 있는
- quick-witted, witty, 재치 있는
- friendly 친절한, 친근한
- adaptable 적응을 잘하는
- passionate, enthusiastic 정열, 열정적인
- diligent, hardworking 근면한, 부지런한
- thoughtful, considerate 생각이 깊은
- creative 창의력 있는
- affable 붙임성 있는, amiable 쾌활한
- easygoing 소탈한, 원만한
- strong-willed 강인한
- warm-hearted 마음이 따뜻한
- dedicated, devoted 헌신적인
- compassionate 인정 많은
- decisive 결단력이 있는

Comprehension Check Exercise

Complete the conversations.

1) A Do you know my friend Joe? B No, ______________________? A He's very tall.	3) A Do you know Fred and Betty? B No, ______________________? A He's tall, and She's very short.
2) A ______________________? B It's very nice. The temperature is mild and good for outdoor activities. So many people go on a picnic or hiking and camping. I love this spring season. These days, It's getting hotter. I feel like summer is coming soon.	4) What is your best friend like? → What does he(she) look like? →

Describing people

General appearance	Height	Hair	Age
What does she look like? →She's tall, with brown hair. →She's pretty. **Does he wear glasses?** →No, he wears contacts.	**How tall is she?** →She's 1 meter 78. **How tall is he?** →He's medium height.	**How long is her hair?** →It's pretty short. **What color is his hair?** →It's dark/light brown.	**How old is she?** →She's about 32. →She's in her thirties. **How old is he?** →He is in his twenties.

A. Write questions to match these statements. Then ask and answer with a partner.

1. → ____?

   A : My brother is 15.

2. → ____?

   A : I'm 164 cm.

3. ➡ ____?

A : My housemate has red hair.

4. ➡ ____?

A : No, he wears contact lenses.

5. ➡ ____?

A : He's medium height and good-looking.

6. ➡ ____?

A : My sister's hair is medium length.

B. **Pair Work** Choose a person in your class. Don't tell your partner who it is. Your partner will ask questions to guess the person's name.

1. What color is his hair?
2. Her hair is medium length.
3. Does she wear a skirt?
4. ….

Modifiers with present participles and prepositions

		Participles
Who's Diego?	He's **the man**	**wearing** a blue shirt.
Which one is Diego?	He's **the one**	**talking** to Brooke.
		Prepositions
Who's Brooke?	She's **the woman**	**with** long black hair.
Which one is Paula?	She **the tall one**	**in** jeans.
Who are the Harrisons?	They're **the people**	**next to** the window.
Which ones are the Harrisons?	They're **the ones**	**on** the couch.

A. Rewrite these statements using modifiers with participles or prepositions.

1. Kyle is the tall guy. He's wearing a red shirt.

   ➡ *Kyle is the tall guy wearing a red shirt.*

2. Mark and Eve are the middle-aged couple. They're talking to Michael.

   ➡ ______________________________.

3. Alexis is the young girl. She's in a white T-shirt and blue jeans.

   ➡ ______________________________.

4. Iris is the woman in the green dress. She's sitting to the left of Mandy.

   ➡ ______________________________.

5. Mac is the serious-looking man. He's playing a chess.

   ➡ ______________________________.

B. **Pair Work** Complete these questions using the given pictures. Then take turns asking and answering the questions.

1. Who's the man sitting next to ______________________________?
2. Who's the woman wearing ______________________________?
3. Who is ______________________________?
4. Which one is ______________________________?
5. Who are the people ______________________________?

04 More Vocabulary & Expression

Vocabulary : Prefixes

Prefixes and some examples of their use

[un]

- unhappy : not happy - The football fans were very unhappy when their team lost.
- uncooked : not cooked - You can't eat these uncooked apples. They are very sour.
- unclean : not clean

[in]

- incomparable
- intolerable : cannot be tolerated or accepted - This heat is intolerable. It's making me feel ill.
- inexpensive : not expensive; cheap - The shop sells inexpensive second-hand computers.
- inactive : not active - He's put on weight because he is so inactive. He should join a gym!

[dis]

- disagree : to not agree - I disagree with my sister about everything.
- disgrace : something to be ashamed of - Your table manners are a disgrace.
- disgusting : so horrible that you feel sick - There's a disgusting smell in the bathroom - open a window, quickly!

A. Build에 관한 표현

■ She is underweight. (negative)	■ She is fat. (negative)
■ She is skinny. (negative)	■ She is overweight. (negative)
■ She is thin. (negative)	■ She is plump. (neutral)
■ She is slim. (positive)	■ She is stocky. (neutral)

B. Beauty에 관한 표현

- Have a defined face (well-defined facial features)
- Have intense eyes
- Have a well-proportioned figure
- She is well-toned.

C. 외모 묘사하기

Can you describe how she looks?

Do you feel she is beautiful? Why?

- I think she **aged gracefully**.
- She has **a well-proportioned and curvy figure**.
- Also, she is **well-toned**.
- I feel she really loves her job and that makes me think that she **has a beautiful mindset**.

- She is **classically beautiful**.
- Even though she is **in her mid fifties**, she is still **at her best.**
- She is **elegant and sophisticated**.

05 Conversation

Situation 1.

A He's got ripped abs. He is quite muscular.
He's in his thirties. Still, he is a great dancer.

B Who are you talking about?

A You know··· He is a member of Shin Hwa.
He is known for his good manners and diligent life style.

B You must be talking about 김동완.

A Right. He is the one.
His name was just on the tip of my tongue.

Situation 2. Job Interview with more Expressions

Interviewer How would you describe yourself?

Interviewee I would describe as a humorous person. I love making people laugh and feel good. I am also a very enthusiastic person and learning and experiencing new things. And I try to have fun in whatever I do. Those efforts give me a lot of energy.

Interviewer I see. Then there must be a lot of friends around you.

Interviewee Yes, you're right, sir. Luckily, I have many friends around me. I enjoy spending time with my friends on weekends.

06 Activities

Describing Physical Appearance

Guess Who?

You are helping to organize a special event at SW University with sports, arts, and *a surprise celebrity guest*. The surprise guest will be invited by vote.

A. Form your group **with 5 members** (including yourself)

B. Choose **one celebrity of them with the good reasons** (There should be advantage for inviting him/her.)

Ex (S)he is known for ~ : ~로 유명하다 (= He is famous for~)

(S)he has ~ : ~을 갖고 있다

(S)he is good at ~ : ~을 잘 한다

C. Describe the celebrity as much as possible.

appearance (Hair, age, looks, height, etc.) using *participles, prepositions,* and *'Be like'* and *'look like'*.

D. The celebrity who has the greatest number in his (/her) described physical appearance will be invited to the special school event!!!!!

*****Don't give the celebrity's name.

07 Job Interview personality

Interviewer : How would you describe yourself?

Key expressions for my answer!

① I am + 형용사. 저는 ~합니다

→ ____.

② I am a(an) 형용사 + person. 저는 ~한 사람입니다

→ ____.

③ I am a person who is + 형용사. 저는 ~한 사람입니다

→ ____.

④ I consider myself (to be) ~. 저는 제가 ~하다고 생각합니다

→ ____.

⑤ My friends (colleagues) tell me that I am ~. 제 친구(동료)들은 제가 ~하다고 합니다

→ ____.

⑥ People say that I have ~. 사람들은 제가 ~하다고 말합니다

→ ____.

⑦ I can define my personality with the word '…' because ~.

나는 ~이기 때문에 … 라는 말로 제 성격을 정의할 수 있습니다

→ ____.

⑧ My personality has been developed by ~ing. 내 성격은 ~에 의해서 길러졌다

→ ____.

Case 1. 유머감각

I have a sense of humor. I love making people laugh and feel good. I am also a very enthusiastic person and learning and experiencing new things. And I try to have fun in whatever I do. Those efforts give me a lot of energy.

저는 유머감각이 있어서 사람들을 웃게 하고 기분 좋게 해주는 것을 좋아합니다. 저는 또한 새로운 것을 배우고 경험하는 것에 대해 매우 열정적입니다. 무엇을 하든지 간에 재미를 찾으려고 합니다. 이러한 노력이 저를 활기 넘치게 합니다.

Case 2. 성실함

I'm a very studious, hardworking person. I do my best to turn in my work completed and get a better result. To do that, every week I organize my thoughts, such as what has been accomplished and what to do next. I know that if I continue to work hard and keep my mind set, I can achieve my goals.

저는 학구적이고 근면하며 단호한 사람입니다. 저는 제 일을 더 잘 수행할 수 있도록 최선을 다합니다. 그래서 매주 생각을 정리하고 지금까지 한 일과 앞으로 해야 할 일들을 정리하는 시간을 갖고 있습니다. 제가 계속 열심히 하고 마음을 굳게 먹는다면 제 목표를 이룰 수 있다고 생각합니다.

Case 3. 적응력

I want to describe myself as an adaptable person. I have stayed in the Philippines for 6 months for studying English. The new environment that I faced was exciting. I could learn and absorb new language-English, while mingling with local friends easily. Because talking to new people and getting to know their culture were enjoyable to me. My personality makes big contribution for when I need to work with many different co-workers and have conversations with various customers.

저는 제 자신을 적응력이 있는 사람이라고 말하고 싶습니다. 영어를 공부하기 위해 6개월간 필리핀에서 지낸 적이 있습니다. 제가 마주한 새로운 경험들은 매우 흥미로웠습니다. 저는 그곳 현지 친구들과 어울려 지내면서 영어를 자연스럽게 습득할 수 있었습니다. 이것은 제가 새로운 사람들을 만나고 그들의 문화를 알아가는 것을 즐겁게 받아들였기 때문이라고 생각합니다. 이러한 제 성격은 다양한 동료들과 함께 일하고 여러 고객들과 대화하는 데 큰 도움이 되고 있습니다.

Case 4. 쾌활, 너그러운 성격

My personality is very cheerful and open-minded as I can approach and talk to new people first in order to create a relaxing atmosphere. I think it has been developed by participating in many school events as a member of student council. Because of my affable manner, I can easily become familiar with new people and build a good relationship with them.

저는 부드러운 분위기를 만들기 위해서 새로운 사람들에게 먼저 다가가고 이야기하는 아주 쾌활하고 너그러운 성격입니다. 제가 보았을 때, 이러한 성격이 대학시절 동안 학생회의 일원으로서 여러 학교 행사에 참여하면서 형성된 것이라고 생각합니다. 저는 붙임성 덕분에 쉽게 많은 사람들과 친해지고 좋은 관계를 유지할 수 있습니다.

Case 5. 체계적, 시간관리

My friends have told me that I am extremely organized and excellent at time management. During our team project, my team members praised me for developing and sticking to a timeline for all the phases of our project. We ended up successfully completing the project ahead of time.

제 친구들은 제가 체계적이고 시간 관리에 뛰어나다고 이야기합니다. 팀 프로젝트를 하는 동안, 저희 팀원들은 제가 프로젝트의 모든 단계에서 일정을 준수하면서 프로젝트를 발전시켜 나가는 것을 칭찬해 주었습니다. 저희는 프로젝트를 예정보다 일찍 성공적으로 마칠 수 있었습니다.

08 TOEIC 문장의 5형식

A. 1형식 : 주어 + 동사

■ 대표적 1형식 동사 : 목적어나 보어를 필요하지 않은 동사(완전자동사) ➟ sing, dance, run, swim, walk, go, come, cry, laugh, depart, arrive, smile, live, work	
그는 춤춘다.	
그는 서울에 간다.	
그녀가 아름답게 웃는다.	
Jackson은 버스를 타고 일하러 간다(출근한다).	

B. 2형식 : 주어 + 동사 + 보어

■ 대표적 2형식 동사 : 보어를 필요로 하고 목적어는 필요하지 않는 동사(불완전자동사) ➟ be, remain, keep, become, grow, get, stay, seem. look, smell, sound, feel, taste	
그 신제품이 매력적이다.	
Kim은 의사가 될 것이다.	
그는 겁에 질려 보인다.	
그거 좋은 의견이다.	

C. 3형식 : 주어 + 동사 + 목적어

■ 자동사 vs. 타동사

■ **대표적 3형식 동사 : 목적어를 필요로 하는 동사를 완전타동사라고 한다. 목적어 위치에는 명사나 명사의 역할을 하는 to부정사, 동명사가 올 수 있다.** ➟ **wish, hope, like, have, want, answer, enjoy, avoid, check, request, provide, receive**	
I want to go to the room.	
He prefers to read a book.	

D. 4형식 : 주어 + 동사 + 간접 목적어 + 직접 목적어

■ **대표적 4형식 동사 : '~에게(간목) …을(직목) 주다'의 의미를 나타내는 동사(수여동사)이다. 4형식 문장은 전치사를 이용해서 3형식 문장으로 변형가능하다.** ➟ **give, offer, buy, teach, tell, send, bring, show**	
그는 나에게 셔츠를 주었다.	
내가 너에게 아이스크림을 사줄게.	
Nick은 그의 아들에게 장난감 집을 만들어 주었다.	

E. 5형식 : 주어 + 동사 + 목적어 + 목적격 보어

■ **대표적 5형식 동사** ➟ **make, find, keep, leave, consider, call, elect, name**	
그녀는 그를 Sam이라고 이름을 지어주었다.	
The smell made everyone hungry.	
문을 그대로 열어두세요.	

01. Employees in that department _______ from 10 A.M. to 6 P.M.

(a) working (b) work

02. Ms. Miller expressed her ______ of the work that the sales team had done.

(a) approve (b) approval (c) approving

03. His dog, Sally will remain _______ until night.

(a) activity (b) active

04. Ms. Rose requested _______ to use the printer.

(a) permitted (b) permission

05. Could someone please _______ the door because it is so cold in here?

(a) close (b) be closed (c) closing

UNIT 03

I like to stay in shape

UNIT GOALS

- Make small talk
- Talk about routines like hobby

GRAMMAR FOCUS

- Present Simple
- Adverbs of frequency

JOB SUCCESS

- TOEIC : RC - 형용사 / 부사
- Job Interview : Hobby

01 Introduction

Most people think that regular exercise is essential, although not everyone does it. They exercise outdoors, at home, or a gym or health club. Many people play sports after school, after work, or on weekends. People exercise for different reasons: to lose weight, to stay in shape, or just to relax.

As for flight attendants, good physical health is one of the crucial qualifications to perform well in an airplane. Applying for a flight attendant job requires the applicant to be in excellent physical health. Flight attendants are exposed to the harsh working environment because of irregular sleeping patterns, as well as standing for extended periods with limited rest periods. To prove that an applicant is in good physical health and can endure the nature of the job, airlines require a medical examination.

Q1. Do you exercise or play sports? → ______________________________

Vocabulary – Sports and exercise

stretching / basketball / jogging / soccer / weight lifting / volleyball / bike riding / golf / martial arts / Pilates / swimming / yoga

Q2. Which activities are used with do, go, or play?

Do martial arts	Go bike riding	Play golf

02 Build Up I

What are some of your morning routines?

03 Conversation

Let' s practice the conversation.

A Which day is your favorite day of the week, Brian?

B Well, I love Fridays.

A Why's that?

B Because it's the last day of the work week. And I usually go to the movies on Friday nights. How about you, Joo?

A I like Mondays.

B Are you serious?

A Yes, I am. I work out on Monday mornings. It puts me in a great mood. Why don't you join me this Monday?

B No, thanks. I will hate Mondays even more then.

Learn more about phrases

- parctice the trumpet
- bake a cake
- drink in a bar
- …
- do judo
- sing karaoke
- play video games

What do you do during the week?

I love to sing karaoke. I go to a karaoke bar with my friends once a week…

On Sundays, I bake with my mother. We bake chocolate cakes…

04 Basic Grammar

Let's learn about the present simple.

	Present simple
Meaning and use	• regular activity • habits • facts and truths • permanent situations
Form - Positive	**subject + verb** They **live** in Rome. Julian **starts** work at nine o'clock and **finishes** at five.
Form - Negative	Junhee **doesn't eat** breakfast every morning.
With adverbs of frequency & time expressions	like **every day, once a week, on Fridays** **I check** my email **every day**. (regular activity) **Sheryl works** at the bank. (permanent situation)
Form - Questions	**Do you read** the news online every day? **Does the supermarket sell** stamps?

Complete the sentences.

1. He ______________________ class on Fridays. (not / have)
2. Mira ______________________ to the store yesterday. (go)
3. I ______________________ around Asia last summer. (travel)
4. We ______________________ three times a week. (exercise)
5. Janie ______________________ her teeth after every meal. (brush)

6. The teacher **(doesn't see / didn't see)** Carolyn in class last week.

7. Do you ______________________________ the guitar every day? **(practice)**

8. Where _________ you _________ every day after class? **(go)**

Take note : spelling changes

In the present simple, regular verbs end in -s or -es, but -y changes to -i.

- marry - marries
- study - studies

➡

05 Grammar Focus

Let's learn about the Adverbs of frequency.

Question

- **How often** do you exercise?

Answer

- I run on the treadmill **every day**.
- I go jogging **once a week**.
- I play soccer **twice a month**.
- I swim about **three times a year**.
- I don't exercise very **often/much**.
- **Usually** I exercise before class.

Question

- Do you **ever** watch TV in the evening?

Answer

- Yes, I **often** watch TV after dinner.
- I **sometimes** watch TV before bed.
- **Sometimes** I watch TV before bed.
- I **hardly ever** watch TV.
- No, I **never** watch TV.

Usually *and* sometimes *can begin a sentence.*

- always
- almost always
- usually
- often
- sometimes
- hardly ever
- almost never
- never

Comprehension Check Exercise

A. Put the adverbs in the correct place. Sometimes there is more than one correct answer. Then practice with a partner.

B. **Pair Work** Take turns asking the questions. Give your own information when answering.

1. A Do you play sports? (ever)
   B Sure. I play soccer. (twice a week)
2. A What do you do on Saturday mornings? (usually)
   B Nothing much. I sleep until noon. (almost always)
3. A Do you lift weights at the gym? (often)
   B No, I lift weights. (hardly ever)
4. A Do you exercise on Sundays? (always)
   B No, I exercise on Sundays. (never)
5. A What do you do after class? (usually)
   B I go out with my classmates. (about three times a week)
6. A Do you go to the movies? (often)
   B Yes, I go to the movies. (once a week)
7. A Do you go bike riding? (ever)
   B No, I ride a bike. (hardly ever)
8. A Do you walk to school? (sometimes)
   B Sure. I walk to school. (five days a week)

Questions with how; short answers

How **often** do you work out?	How **well** do you play tennis?
▪ Every day. ▪ Twice a week. ▪ Not very often.	▪ Pretty well. ▪ About average. ▪ Not very well.

How **long** do you spend at the gym?	How **good** are you at sports?
▪ Thirty minutes a day. ▪ Two hours a week. ▪ About an hour on weekends.	▪ Pretty good. ▪ OK. ▪ Not so good.

Comprehension Check Exercise

Complete these questions. Then practice with a partner.

1. A ________________ at sports?
   B I guess I'm pretty good. I play a lot of different sports.
2. A ________________ spend online?
   B About an hour after dinner. I like to chat with my friends.
3. A ________________ go to the beach?
   B Once or twice a month. It's a good way to relax.
4. A ________________ swim?
   B Not very well. I need to take swimming lessons.

06 Pair Activity

Activity 1

A. Find out about your partner's daily life using the questions below. Record your partner's answers in the chart and ask follow-up questions to gain more information.

Do you···	Yes, always	Yes, often	Yes, sometimes	No, hardly ever	No, never	Extra information
have a big breakfast?						
wash your hair?						
arrive late to class?						
exercise?						
read a news website?						
go shopping?						
drink coffee in the morning?						
have lunch with friends?						
go to bed before 11 p.m?						

B. Now, tell the class what you found out about your partner, include the extra information.

→ He/She always (often, sometimes, hardly ever, never) ···

Activity 2

	See your best friend	Get angry	Eat chocolate	Go away for the weekend	Do sport or exercise

- Go to the bed before 11p.m.
- Go to the hairdresser's
- Hang out with friends
- Listen to the music
- Arrive late to class
- Drink coffee
- Go to the parties
- Wear jeans

Cook your own dinner	Have lunch with friends	Visit relatives	Use public transportation	Forget something important	Feel lazy

How often do you work out?

- **Every day.**
- **Twice a week.**
- **Not very often.**

How well do you play tennis?

- **Pretty well.**
- **About average.**
- **Not very well.**

How long do you spend at the gym?

- **Thirty minutes a day.**
- **Two hours a week.**
- **About an hour on weekends.**

How good are you at sports?

- **Pretty good.**
- **OK.**
- **Not so good.**

100%

- always
- almost always
- usually
- often
- sometimes
- hardly ever
- almost never
- never

0%

- From time to time
- Every morning / day / week
- Once / twice / three times a day
- Once / twice / three times a week
- Once / twice / three times a month

07 TOEIC 형용사/부사

형용사의 형태와 역할

A. 형용사의 개념 및 형태

B. 형용사의 역할

C. 〈be + 형용사 + 전치사〉 구문

부사의 형태와 역할

A. 부사의 개념 및 형태

B. 부사의 역할

C. 기타 중요 부사

01. The room is completely ______ right now.

(a) empty (b) fully

02. The benefits package for GIA Corp. workers is ______ .

(a) attractive (b) attractively

03. Mr. Lincoln ______ completed the work process for meeting the due date.

(a) fully (b) full

04. This year's music award will be ______ the same as last year's.

(a) entirely (b) entire

05. There will be ______ rain from noon to midnight the day after tomorrow.

(a) heavily (b) heavy (c) heaviness

08 Job Interview Hobby

Question What is your hobby?

= What kind of hobbies do you have? / What do you do in your spare time? / What do you do when you meet your friends?

단순한 여가활동, 취미를 설명하기에 그치지 말고 그것으로 사람들과의 관계를 형성해 나가는 모습, 팀워크, 밝고 진취적인 모습 등을 보여주는게 좋다.
영화나 책을 말하게 될 경우, 줄거리 설명하다보면 영어 실력의 한계에 부딪힐 수 있으므로, 줄거리는 간략하게 소개하고 영화를 보면서 느낀점이나 인상적이었던 장면, 시사하고자 하는 점, 대사에 대해서 말하는 편이 좋다.

key expressions! - 운동, 취미관련

I work out ~ ~운동합니다.

- I work out every other day. 이틀에 한번 운동
- I work out at a gym by my place. 집근처 헬스장
- I work out by using the treadmill. 런닝머신 이용

I try to ~ ~하려고 노력합니다.

- I try to exercise on a regular basis. 규칙적으로 운동
- I try to maintain healthy eating habits. 건강한 식습관
- I try to walk rather than drive. 운전보다는 걷는 습관

One of my favorite hobbies is ~ 제가 가장 좋아하는 취미는 ~입니다.

- One of my favorite hobbies is traveling. 여행입니다
- One of my favorite hobbies is going to the movies. 영화감상입니다
- One of my favorite hobbies is reading books. 독서입니다

In my spare time, I like ~ing 저는 여가시간에 ~하는 것을 좋아합니다.

- In my spare time, I like going on a picnic with my family. 가족 소풍
- In my spare time, I like going to the beach and relax. 여행

I enjoy ~ing in my free time 저는 여가시간에 ~하는 것을 즐깁니다.

- I enjoy playing badminton with my father in my free time.
  아버지와 함께 배드민턴 치는 것을 즐깁니다.
- I enjoy going to the bookstore to buy a new bestseller in my free time.
  새로 나온 베스트셀러 사기 위해 서점가는 것을 즐깁니다.

It's a good(great) way to ~ ~하는데 좋습니다.

- It's a good way to unwind when not at work. 오프데이 때 긴장 푸는
- It's a good way to stay in shape. 건강 유지하는
- It's a good way to spice up your routine. 일상을 더욱 즐겁게
- It's a good way to increase my fitness levels steadily. 체력 꾸준히 단련
- It's a good way to relieve stress. 스트레스 해소
- It's a good way to spend time by myself. 혼자서 시간 보내기에
- It's a good way to relax and have fun. 휴식 취하고 즐겁게 보내기에

useful expression!

- take a break 휴식하다
- take a walk 산책하다
- take my dog for a walk 강아지 산책시키다
- read books 독서하다
- go to the movies 영화보다
- listen to music 음악 듣다
- play tennis(sports) 테니스(스포츠)를 하다
- work out 운동하다
- do yoga 요가하다
- enjoy delicious food 맛있는 음식을 먹다
- enjoy cultural life 문화생활을 즐기다
- ride a bike 자전거 타다
- hang out with friends 친구들과 어울리다
- do absolutely nothing 아무것도 하지 않다
- surf the net 인터넷을 검색하다
- go for a drive 드라이브 하다
- try out different restaurant 여러 식당에서 음식 먹어보다
- play the piano(musical instrument) 피아노, 악기를 연주하다
- go ~ing(fishing, camping, swimming, hiking) (낚시, 캠핑, 수영, 하이킹)하러 가다

Answer Case 1. 여행

Traveling is one of my favorite hobbies. I love visiting famous places, seeing historical sites, and experiencing new cultures and people. Taking pictures to keep memorable moments is one of the great joys. After returning from this trip, I print the photos and make a note about the trip. Traveling definitely gives me much pleasure.

여행은 제가 가장 좋아하는 취미 중 하나입니다. 저는 유명한 곳을 방문하고, 유적지를 보고, 새로운 문화와 사람들을 경험하는 것을 좋아합니다. 기억에 남는 순간을 간직하기 위해 사진을 찍는 것은 큰 기쁨 중 하나입니다. 이번 여행에서 돌아온 후 사진을 인쇄하고 여행에 대한 메모를 합니다. 여행은 확실히 나에게 많은 즐거움을 줍니다.

Case 2. 요가하기

Nowadays, my interest is all about health care. One of the things I am into is yoga. I like it because although it requires many kinds of positions and movements, it is not too difficult. Even when days are tough, yoga allows me to let go of the things that were on my mind and gain a sense of calm.

요즘 제 관심은 온통 건강관리에 쏠려 있습니다. 제가 좋아하는 것 중 하나는 요가입니다. 여러 가지 자세와 동작이 필요하지만 그다지 어렵지 않기 때문에 좋아합니다. 힘든 날에도 요가를 하면, 마음에 담아 두던 것들을 풀어주고 마음의 평안을 얻을 수 있게 해줍니다.

Case 3. 만들기

I just like making things in general. I definitely gravitate toward hobbies that require creativity. I have joined a handcraft club, so I've got to meet many people with a common interest regularly. Coming up with new arts and sharing craft ideas with club members are always fun for me. Recently I have given my friends some of my handcraft as gifts. It's my everyday happiness to see my friends be surprised and happy to receive gifts.

저는 일반적으로 만드는 걸 좋아합니다. 저는 분명히 창의력이 필요한 취미에 끌립니다. 저는 수공예 동호회에 가입했기 때문에, 정기적으로 공통의 관심을 가진 많은 사람들을 만나고 있습니다. 새로운 예술품을 고안하고 클럽 회원들과 공예 아이디어를 공유하는 것은 저에게 항상 즐겁습니다. 최근에 저는 친구들에게 제 수공예품을 선물해 주었습니다. 친구들이 깜짝 놀라며 선물을 받는 모습을 보는 것이 일상의 행복입니다.

Case 4. 맛집 탐방

I like to try out famous restaurants and have tasty dishes with my friends. While enjoying food, as most girlfriends do, we just love talking about our routine lives and taking pictures of the food. I also upload the photos and post reviews on my SNS. It's great fun to explore new restaurants and to share tasty meals with friends.

저는 친구들과 함께 유명한 레스토랑을 둘러보고 맛있는 음식을 먹는 것을 좋아합니다. 대부분의 여자친구들이 그렇듯이, 음식을 즐기면서, 우리는 그저 일상생활에 대해 이야기하고 음식을 사진 찍는 것을 좋아합니다. 사진을 올리고 SNS에 리뷰를 올리기도 합니다. 새로운 레스토랑을 탐험하고 친구들과 맛있는 식사를 함께 하는 것은 매우 즐겁습니다.

Case 5. 노래 부르기

I like singing very much. There is the 'coin singing room' in Korea. Once I take several coins, I can get ready to sing and dance, listening to K-pop. When I am a bit depressed, singing makes me feel much better. Moreover, sometimes when I have a companion who shares this hobby with me, I love to go singing room with them. It's amusing.

저는 노래하는 것을 매우 좋아합니다. 한국에는 '코인 노래방'이 있습니다. 동전을 여러 개 가져가면 K팝을 들으면서 노래하고 춤출 준비를 할 수 있습니다. 좀 우울한 날에 노래를 부르면 기분이 훨씬 좋아집니다. 게다가, 가끔 이 취미를 같이 하는 친구가 있을 때, 저는 친구들과 노래방에 가는 것을 좋아합니다. 매우 재미있습니다.

Case 6. 영화 보기

I love to go to the movies. I have a friend who shares this hobby with me. We like watching all types of films. Once the film is over, we discuss it together. It's quite fun to share different views. Moreover, I love being inside and sitting back in the theater. That makes me feel very relaxed.

저는 영화 보러 가는 것을 좋아합니다. 이 취미를 같이 하는 친구가 있습니다. 우리는 모든 장르의 영화를 좋아합니다. 영화가 끝나면 함께 이야기 하는데, 서로 다른 견해를 이야기 하는 것은 꽤 재미있습니다. 게다가, 저는 극장 안에서 편하게 앉아 있는 것을 좋아합니다. 영화관에서 영화를 보면 마음이 편해집니다.

Case 7. 조깅하기

My favorite activity is jogging. In my opinion, jogging is an excellent exercise in many ways. It is, of course, a typical aerobic exercise, so doing some cardio helps me burn some extra calories and stay in shape. Besides, by doing this, I could enjoy the fresh air and seeing other people and dogs. Also, it gives me refreshment and time with myself. While enjoying it, I could organize my thoughts, such as what has been accomplished and what to do next week.

제가 가장 좋아하는 활동은 조깅입니다. 조깅은 여러 면에서 훌륭한 운동이라고 생각합니다. 물론, 이 운동은 대표적인 유산소 운동이기 때문에, 여분의 칼로리를 소모하고 몸매를 유지하는데 도움을 줍니다. 게다가 운동하면서 신선한 공기를 마실 수도 있고 다른 사람들과 개들도 구경할 수 있습니다. 또 그것은 기분전환과 생각을 정리할 수 있게 해줍니다. 저는 성취한 것들과 다음 주에 해야 할 것 같은 생각을 정리할 수 있었습니다.

UNIT 04

What to wear

• UNIT GOALS

- Talk about what they are doing and wearing now

• GRAMMAR FOCUS

- Present Continuous

• JOB SUCCESS

- TOEIC : LC - 사진 묘사

01 Introduction

I just play it safe

3 Questions Put the words in the correct order to make sentences about Mandy.

01. What does she do?

at	working	is	works	this	in	She	university

A : ______________________________.

02. What does she normally wear for work?

normally	is	wears	wearing	She	formal suits	for work

A : ______________________________.

03. What is she wearing now?

is	a	are	dark blue	wears	some	wearing	She	suit

A : ____.

Other Questions

04. What does she wear at the weekends?

05. What is her favorite fashion item? And why?

02 Build Up

Answer the following questions to build up the sentence.

She is wearing a dark blue suit now.

A. Did she wear a dark blue suit last week?

B. Will she wear a dark blue suit next week?

C. What comes before and after the word of 'wear'?

D. What is ________ wearing now?

E. What are you and your classmates wearing now?

F. Is ________ wearing a gold ring now?

Exercise **Who is scruffy- and who is smart?**

Hi, my name's Charlotte. I work in branding.
Right now I'm wearing a grey jumper, some black jeans and some black trainers.
I am quite scruffy but normally I wear smarter clothes.
But at the weekend, I'm smart casual.

My name's Ed. I'm a graphic designer.
I'm wearing a red hoodie, some black jeans and some grey trainers.
For work, I wear casual clothes, occasionally smart clothes. It's alright if I wear scruffy clothes at work, as long as it's not every day.
Yeah - at weekends I wear jeans and a t-shirt as well.

Questions

A. Who is wearing grey trainers?

B. What does Charlotte wear at weekends?

C. Who says they're wearing scruffy clothes?

D. What is the casually dressed person's job

Next

So Charlotte said she's 'quite scruffy' today. How about you? What kind of clothes do you like to wear - smart, casual or smart casual? And what is your favorite fashion item?

03 More Expressions

사진 보고 패션 표현하기

She paired ripped jeans with a black t shirt.

And she threw on a jacket.

The color of the jacket is vivid.

It's a floral patterned jacket.

The jacket brightens her look.

It's a feminine and dressy look.

She paired a white form-fitting dress with ankle strap heels.

She has a curvy figure and her white dress accentuates her curves.

Especially, she is wearing a black belt and it accentuates her waist.

04 Conversation

Let's practice the conversation.

A Hello.

B Jim, what are you doing? Are you still sleeping? You're late for work!

A No, I'm not sleeping. **I'm not feeling well today**.

B Are you sick?

A Yeah.

B What's wrong?

A I **have** a headache, a cough, and a fever. So I'm just resting at home.

B Oh, you **have** the flu. I am sorry to hear that. I hope you will get better soon.

A Thank you. **I'm sure I'll** be better by tomorrow. I just need some rest.

B By the way, **are you done with** your work for the meeting tomorrow?

A Almost. Paul is going to cover for me.

B Okay. Take good care of yourself.

Vocabulary :

A. Learn about common illnesses and symptoms.

cough	fever	headache
runny nose	sneeze	sore throat

- I have a cold. / I have the flu.
  - N + ache : head**ache**, tooth**ache**, back**ache**, stomach**ache**
  - sore + N : **sore** throat, **sore** muscles

B. Complete the sentences with the correct words.

1. The boy's body temperature is 39. He has a ________________.
2. Kelly neeks to see a dentist. She has a ________________.
3. This tea is good for a ________________.
4. A Why are you wearing a mask?

   B I have a ________________. I am sneezing a lot.

Pattern Training :

A. I'm sure I'll ________________. 제가 ~할 거라고 확신합니다.

1. do a good job → 잘 해낼 것이라고
2. be a valuable asset to your company → 당신의 회사에 귀중한 자산이 될 것이라고
3. succeed → 성공할 것이라고

B. Are you done with ________________? ~을 마쳤습니까?

1. the report → 보고서
2. your dinner → 저녁식사
3. the newspaper → 신문 (신문 읽기를)

05 Basic Grammar

Grammar point : Present Continuous Tense

Learn about the present continuous tense.

I **am** watch**ing** TV. We **are** hav**ing** dinner.	She **isn't** study**ing** English. You **aren't** do**ing** well.	**Is** James play**ing** soccer? **Are** they clean**ing** the house?

PAIR ACTIVITY : Present Continuous Party

In this activity, you assume the identity of someone at a party and talk about their current activities. You begin by giving and answering questions on the card. You walk around and speak to the other partygoers in their group.

The students ask each other the questions from the role card and write the answers down in a chart on their worksheet using the third person singular. When everyone has finished, students report back to the class on the people they met at the party.

Name : ____________________

Your job : I am a DJ.

What are you doing at the party?

I ____________ (play) music.

What are you doing right now?

Are you enjoying the party?

Yes/No, I am having a ________ time,

Because ____________________

____

Name : ____________________

Your job : I am an actor/actress.

What are you doing at the party?

I ____________ (meet) some friends.

What are you doing right now?

Are you enjoying the party?

Yes/No, I am having a ________ time,

Because ____________________

____

Name : ____________________

Your job : I am a photographer.

What are you doing at the party?

I ________ (take) photos for a magazine.

What are you doing right now?

Are you enjoying the party?

Yes/No, I am having a ________ time,

Because ____________________

____

Name : ____________________

Your job : I am a singer.

What are you doing at the party?

I __________ (promote) my new song.

What are you doing right now?

Are you enjoying the party?

Yes/No, I am having a ________ time,

Because ____________________

____

Name : ______________________

Your job : I am a guitarist.

What are you doing at the party?

I ______________ (play) music.

What are you doing right now?

Are you enjoying the party?

Yes/No, I am having a ________ time,

Because ______________________

____

Name : ______________________

Your job : I am a waiter/waitress.

What are you doing at the party?

I ______________ (serve) food and drink.

What are you doing right now?

Are you enjoying the party?

Yes/No, I am having a ________ time,

Because ______________________

____

Name : ______________________

Your job : I am a student.

What are you doing at the party?

I ______________ (have) birthday party.

What are you doing right now?

Are you enjoying the party?

Yes/No, I am having a ________ time,

Because ______________________

____

Name : ______________________

Your job : I am a flight attendant.

What are you doing at the party?

I ______________ (have) a social gathering.

What are you doing right now?

Are you enjoying the party?

Yes/No, I am having a ________ time,

Because ______________________

____

06 Grammar Focus

Let's learn and compare
: Present simple vs. Present continuous

	Present simple	Present continuous
Meaning & Use	• regular activity • facts and truths • habits • permanent situations	• things that are happening now at the time we are speaking, • temporary situations • activities that are in progress
Form Positive / Negative	**subject + verb** *They **live** in Rome.* *Julian**starts** work at nine o'clock and **finishes** at five.*	**subject + am, are, is + verb-ing** *Can I call you back later? We**'re having*** dinner right now.
With adverbs of frequency & time expressions	like **every day, once a week, on Fridays** ***I check** my email **every day**.* (regular activity) ***Sheryl works** at the bank.* (permanent situation)	like **at the moment, today, this week** *Just a minute. I**'m checking** my email.* (now) *She usually works in London, but she**'s working** from home this* week. (temporary situation) *I**'m studying** Economics* (activity in progress)
Form - Questions	***Do you read** the news online every day?* ***Does the supermarket sell** stamps?*	*What **are you doing**?* ***Is it raining**?*

Take note : spelling changes

In the present simple, regular verbs end in -s or -es, but -y changes to -i.

- *marry - marries*
- *study - studies*

In the present continuous, all verbs end in -ing, but sometimes the spelling changes.

- *make - making*
- *sit - sitting*
- *die - dying*

Take note : verbs we don't use in the present continuous

There are some verbs that we don't usually use in the continuous form. They are often verbs linked to the senses and thinking, for example : **hear, see, smell, hate, know, understand, believe, want, need.**

- **Wrong** : *Could you explain that again?* **I'm not understanding.**
- **Correct** : *Could you explain that again?* **I don't understand.**

Comprehension Check Exercise

Match questions 1-8 with answers ⓐ - ⓗ.

1 Does it snow in the UK?	ⓐ My home's in Brazil.
2 Is it snowing in the UK?	ⓑ Yes, I'm the managing director.
3 Do you work here?	ⓒ No, I've got a day off.
4 Are you working today?	ⓓ Just coke, usually.
5 Where do you live?	ⓔ It's water.
6 Where are you living?	ⓕ In a friend's flat in London.
7 What do you drink?	ⓖ Not right now.
8 What are you drinking?	ⓗ Only in winter.

07 Activities

Activity 1.

The Mayor of San Ronaldo

It's not always black and white···

In this activity you're going to do some more practice with antonyms. But first, consider the word old. What is its opposite? Well, it could be new or young. It depends on whether you're thinking of a person or a thing. And what about hard? If you're talking about a surface, the opposite is soft. If you're talking about an exam, the opposite is··· easy. So, each word can have more than one antonym.

Does that make sense? OK, let's put this knowledge to the test!

Read the text and complete the activity

To do

Imagine you live in the beautiful, ancient European city of San Ronaldo. It's time for the city to choose a new mayor, and the two candidates have very different visions for the city. One thinks it should keep its old-fashioned **charm** and focus on tourism; the other believes the only way to succeed is to **modernise**.

So, we begin with a speech from candidate number one.

After that, you have to complete the speech by candidate number two, who disagrees with everything the first one said. In other words, it's a great opportunity to practise antonyms!

Candidate one's speech

"I love San Ronaldo. It's a beautiful city. And that's its biggest advantage. Our narrow streets are perfect for cafes and galleries. We appeal to older tourists with more money. It's hard to see why we should change. We need to remain a traditional town - this is our biggest strength."

Candidate two's speech

Activity 2.

Now you know all about present simple and present continuous. So, you're ready to see some language in action – and test what you know!

Take a look at this article about the colour red and its importance in fashion. We put some mistakes into the article to test you – can you spot them?

There is one mistake in each paragraph. That's 7 mistakes altogether. Each mistake is related to present simple and/or present continuous.

The power of red

It's London Fashion Week. The worlds' **fashionistas** are blogging, tweeting and instagramming about this season's looks and trends to a fashion-hungry audience. The color of the moment is red – bright, bold and brave. In the language of clothing, red makes a statement. For some people, it stands for power; for others, red is meaning danger. But where do these meanings come from – and is the power of the color red changing?

Nowadays, when it comes to color, most of us are wear what we choose. But things were very different back in 15th century England, when only the rich and powerful – and their servants - were allowed to wear the color red – and the English King Henry VIII passed four separate laws to make sure everyone obeyed the rules.

But why the color red? Professor Lisa Jardine of University College, London, is say that the answer is all about money, power and **status**. The **dyes** that turned cloth red in Henry's day were expensive – so only rich people could afford to wear red clothing. Henry's laws were a way of controlling who was able to show their **wealth**, power and social status.

But red had other, more negative meanings - especially for women. The English phrase 'scarlet woman' describe a woman who has lots of sexual partners – so perhaps it doesn't come as a surprise to learn that Queen Elizabeth I (also known as 'The Virgin Queen') often wore white as a symbol of her **purity** – and Queen Elizabeth II wore a white dress for her **coronation**.

But times are changing, and these days, in western fashion at least, women can wear their favorite shade of red without fear. Even the Queen is wearing red on public occasions, and red is one of the Duchess of Cambridge's favorite colors.

So, fashionable women definitely wearing red this September. According to Vogue Magazine, "these reds are healthy, warm and **vibrant**, proving fashion's heart beats strong and sure." There are even some red wedding dresses on show – although I'm not expecting to see them in my local church any time soon…

I'm no scarlet woman, but I think about buying a pair of red boots for myself this winter. After all, if Princess Kate is wearing red this season - that's good enough for me!

This article is based on an original BBC Magazine article.

08 TOEIC 사진묘사

다음 문장을 완성하고, 사진을 묘사하는 문장을 찾으세요.

A.

1. 웨이터는 음식을 서빙하고 있다.
   - The waiter ______________________ a dish.
2. 테이블에 접시가 서빙되고 있다.
   - A dish ______________________ at their table.
3. 두 손님은 와인잔을 들고 있다.
   - Two customers ______________________ their wine glasses.
4. 가스레인지에서 음식이 조리되고 있다.
   - Food ______________________ on the stove.
5. 웨이터가 손님들의 주문을 받고 있다.
   - The waiter ______________________ the customers' orders.

B.

1 모든 사람이 같은 곳을 바라보고 있다.

► All of the people ______________________ in the same direction.

2 한 여자가 컴퓨터에 무언가를 타이핑하고 있다.

► One woman ______________________ something on her laptop.

3 한 남자가 전화기를 손에 쥐고 있다.

► The man ______________________ a telephone in his hand.

4 남자는 정장을 입고 있다.

► The man ______________________ a formal suit.

5 사람들은 모두 서 있다.

► All people in this room ______________________ .

UNIT 05

What did you do last weekend?

• UNIT GOALS

- Talk about past events

• GRAMMAR FOCUS

- Past Simple
- Past Continuous

• JOB SUCCESS

- TOEIC : RC - 동사의 시제 1
- Job Interview : Small Talk

01 Introduction

Check(☑) the activities you do in your free time. List three other activities you do in your free time. What are your favorite free-time activities? Are there activities you don't like? Which ones?

Let's practice the conversation.

A Hey, Pat. It's nice to see you again. How was your winter break?

B It was great, Sam. I went to Mexico.

A Mexico? Why did you go there?

B I volunteered there. We built an elementary school.

A That sounds great.

B I was. How about you? What did you do?

A I went home for the break.

B That sounds nice. Did you spend time with your family and friends?

A Yes, I did on the weekends. I was busy during the week. I worked at a nice restaurant. It was hard work, but I made a lot of money.

B Oh, cool!

TIPS

It's nice to meet you. (Say this the first time you meet someone.)

It's nice to see you (again). (Say this when you see the person again.)

PAIR ACTIVITY

Practice each conversation again. You can use your own stories or different ideas.

02 Warm Up Activity

A. Find more words or phrases from the list that usually go with each verb. And add one more word or phrase to each verb.

a lot of fun	dancing	a good time	shopping	a bike riding
fishing	sightseeing	rock climbing	hiking	camping
the bed	chores	the laundry	a trip	skiing / snow boarding

do	*my homework*			
go	*surfing*			
have	*a party*			
make	*a phone call*			
take	*a day off*			

B. **Group work** Choose the things you did last weekend. Then compare and share it with your partners.

Question **What did you do last weekend?**

Ex **A** I went shopping with my friends. We had a good time. What about you?

B I didn't have a very good time. I did chores.

C I did chores, too. But I went dancing in the evening, and ……

03 Conversation

Step 1. Check the questions before reading the conversation.

Step 2. Then, read the conversation with your partner and ask and answer questions together.

Question 1. **What did Cara do last weekend?**
What did Neil do last weekend?

NEIL So, what did you do last weekend, Cara?

CARA Oh, I had a great time. My friends and I had pizza on Saturday and then we all went dancing.

NEIL How fun! Did you go to The Treadmill?

CARA No, we didn't. We went to that new place downtown. How about you? Did you go anywhere?

NEIL No, I didn't go anywhere all weekend. I just stayed home and studied for today's Spanish test.

CARA Our test is today? I forgot about that!

NEIL Don't worry. You always get an A.

Question 2. **What does Cara do on Sunday afternoons?**

NEIL So, Cara, what did you do on Sunday?

CARA I stayed home in the morning. I just watched TV and read.

NEIL How about in the afternoon?

CARA Oh, I worked. I have a part-time job at the university bookstore.

NEIL I didn't know you had a job.

CARA Yeah, I'm a cashier there. I work every Sunday from 1:00 to 6:00.

PAIR ACTIVITY

Think about what you did last weekend. Then share it with your partners.

Question **What did you do last weekend?**

Ex
A I went shopping with my friends. We had a good time. What about you?

B I didn't have a very good time. I did chores.

C I did chores, too. But I went dancing in the evening, and ……

04 Basic Grammar

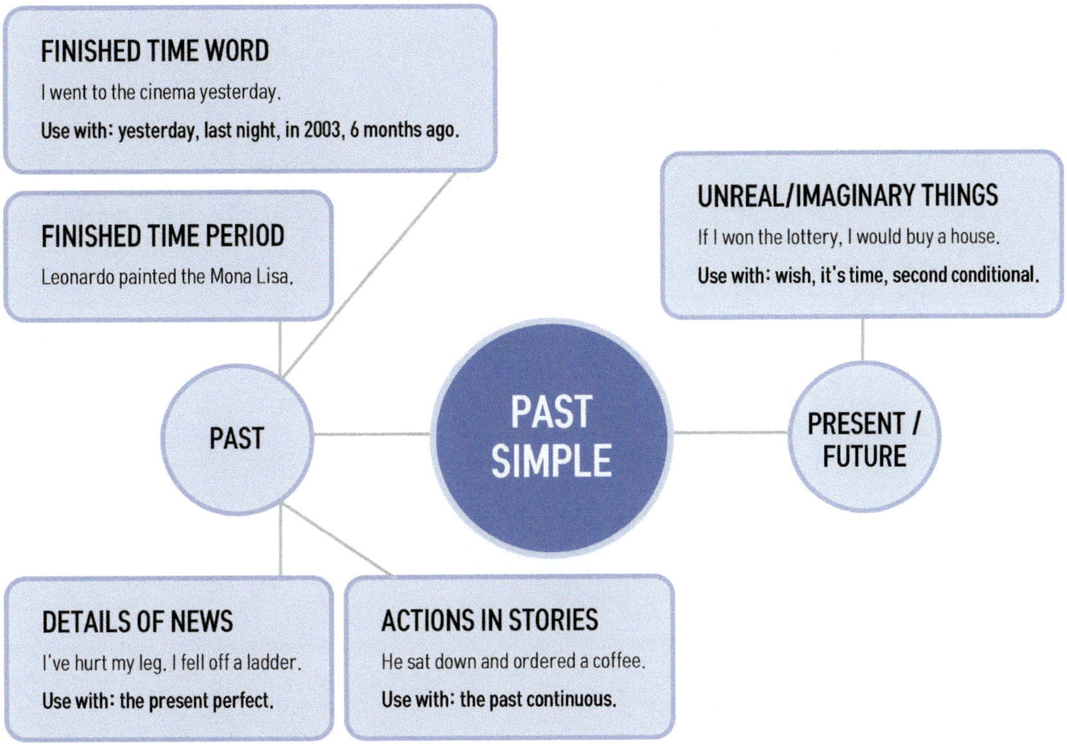

Let's learn about Simple past.

Did you **work** on Saturday?	What **did** Neil **do** on Saturday?
▪ Yes, I **did.** I **worked** all day. ▪ No, **I didn't.** I **didn't work** at all.	▪ He **stayed** home and **studied** for a test.
Did you **go** anywhere last weekend?	How **did** Cara **spend** her weekend?
▪ Yes, I **did.** I **went** to the movies. ▪ No, I **didn't.** I **didn't go** anywhere.	▪ She **went** to a club and **danced** with some friends.

Comprehension Check Exercise 1

A. Complete these questions. Then practice with a partner.

1. **A** _______ you _______ (stay) home on Sunday?

   B No, I _______ (call) my friend Anna. We _______ (drive) to a nice little restaurant for lunch.

2. **A** How _______ you _______ (spend) your last birthday?

   B I _______ (have) a party. Everyone _______ (enjoy) it, but the neighbors next door _______ (not, like) the noise.

3. **A** What _______ you _______ (do) last night?

   B I _______ (see) a sci-fi movie at the Cineplex. I _______ (love) it! Amazing special effects!

4. **A** _______ you _______ (do) anything special over the weekend?

   B Yes, I _______ . I _______ (go) shopping. Unfortunately, I _______ (spend) all my money. Now I'm broke!

5. **A** _______ you _______ (go) out on Friday night?

   B No, I _______ . I _______ (invite) friends over, and I _______ (cook) spaghetti for them.

regular verbs	▪ work → worked	▪ invite → invited	
	▪ study → studied	▪ stop → stopped	
irregular verbs	▪ buy → bought	▪ do → did	▪ drive → drove
	▪ have → had	▪ go → went	▪ sing → sang
	▪ see → saw	▪ spend → spent	

B. **Pair Work** Take turns asking the questions in part A. Give your own information when answering.

Ex **A** Did you stay home on Sunday?

B No, I didn't. I went dancing with some friends.

Let's learn about Past of be.

A. Complete these questions. Then practice with a partner.

Were you in Califonia?	Yes, I **was.**
Was the weather OK?	No, it **wasn't.**
Were you and your cosin on vacation?	Yes, we **were.**
Were your parents there?	No, they **weren't.**
How long **were** you away?	I **was** away for a week.
How **was** your vacation?	It **was** excellent!

Comprehension Check Exercise 2

Complete these questions. Then practice with a partner.

1. A ________ you in New York weekend?
   B No, I ________. I ________ in Chicago.
   A How ________ it?
   B It ________ great! But it ________ cold and windy as usual.

2. A How long ________ your parents in Chile?
   B They ________ there for two weeks.
   A ________ they in Santiago the whole time?
   B No, they ________. They also went to Valparaiso.

3. A ________ you away last week?
   B Yes, I ________ in Madrid.
   A Really? How long ________ you there?
   B For almost a week. I ________ there on business.

05 Speaking Exercise

Question What did you do last weekend?

When I __________ (wake up) in the morning, the sun __________ (shine), and the birds __________ (sing). So, I __________ (go to) the park near my place to take a walk with my daughter. While we __________ (walk) along the Han River, I suddenly __________ (feel) hungry. So we __________ (drop by) the café. People __________ laughing and chatting. We __________ (sit) down and ordered some drinks and light food. Everything was perfect. I guess my daughter felt happy. On the way back home, she __________ constantly __________ (sing).

06 Grammar Focus

Look at these examples to see how the past continuous and past simple are used.

When I woke up this morning, it was snowing.

I was sleeping when you called me.

Grammar explanation

Past simple

A. The past simple shows us that an action was in the past, not in the present. Regular past simple verbs have -ed at the end (e.g. *called, played, arrived*). Irregular verbs have a different form, usually with a different vowel sound (e.g. *wake → woke, break → broke, feel → felt*).

- My parents called me yesterday.
- I woke up early this morning.
- Sam played basketball when he was at university.

B. We make the negative with didn't and the infinitive verb.

- My parents didn't call me yesterday.
- I didn't wake up early this morning.

C. We make the question form with did and then the subject and infinitive verb.

- Did you wake up early this morning?
- Did Sam play basketball when he was at university?

Past continuous

A. The past continuous shows us that the action was already in progress at a certain time in the past.

- What were you doing at 8 p.m. last night? I was studying.

→ This means that I started studying before 8 p.m. and I continued after 8 p.m.

B. The past continuous can also show that an activity was in progress for some time, not just for a moment.

- We were cleaning the house all morning.

C. We make the past continuous with *was* or *were* and the *-ing* form of the verb.

- She couldn't come to the party. She was working.
- Three years ago, we were living in my home town.
- I tried to give him some advice, but he wasn't listening.
- What were you doing this time last year?

Past continuous and past simple

A. When we use these two tenses together, it shows us that the past simple action happened in the middle of the past continuous action, while it was in progress.

- While I was studying, I suddenly felt sleepy.

B. We often use these tenses to show an action interrupting another action.

- I broke my leg when I was skiing.
- As I was going to work, I saw an old friend.
- We were watching television when the power went off.

Can you see a difference in the meaning of these two sentences?

- When the guests arrived, Jane was cooking dinner.
- When the guests arrived, Jane cooked dinner.

In the first one, Jane started cooking dinner before the guests arrived. We know that because it uses the past continuous. In the second sentence, the guests arrived first and then Jane started cooking.

PAST CONTINUOUS

OVERLAPPING ACTION
I was walking to the station when I met John.
Use with: when + past simple, two o'clock, 7pm.

STORY BACKGROUND
The birds were singing and the sun was shining. Amy sat down.
Use with: the past simple.

SOME PAST HABITS
She was constantly singing.
Use with: always, forever, constantly, at that time, in those days.

EMPHASIS OF LENGTH OF ACTION
I was working in the garden all day.
Use with: all day, all evening, for hours.

Comprehension Check Exercise

1. What _______ (you/do) when I _______ (call) you last night?
2. I _______ (sit) in a café when you _______ (call).
3. When you _______ (arrive) at the party, who _______ (be) there?
4. Susie _______ (watch) a film when she _______ (hear) the noise.
5. Yesterday I ______ (go) to the library, next I ______ (have) a swimming lesson, later I _______ (meet) Julie for a coffee.
6. We _______ (play) tennis when John _______ (hurt) his ankle.
7. What _______ (they/do) at 10pm last night? It _______ (be) really noisy.
8. He _______ (take) a shower when the telephone _______ (ring).
9. He _______ (be) in the shower when the telephone _______ (ring).
10. When I _______ (walk) into the room, everyone _______ (work).
11. It _______ (be) a day last September. The sun _______ (shine), the birds _______ (sing). I ______ (walk) along the street when I ______ (meet) an old friend.
12. He _______ (live) in Russia when the Revolution _______ (start).
13. When her train ______ (get) to the station, we ______ (wait) on the platform.
14. He ______ (be) so annoying! He ______ (always/leave) his things everywhere.
15. On holiday we _______ (visit) Rome, _______ (see) the Vatican, and _______ (spend) a few days at the beach.
16. Why _______ (you/stand) on a chair when I _______ (come) into the room?
17. They _______ (live) in Germany when they _______ (be) young.
18. At 7pm yesterday, we _______ (listen) to music.
19. When I _______ (leave) the house, it _______ (snow).
20. He _______ (work) in a bank when he _______ (meet) his wife.

07 Listening

I was on vacation

A. Listen to Daniel and Amanda talk about their vacations.

(Refer to Dialogue on next page)

Did they have a good time? Check(☑) Yes or No.

	Yes	No
Daniel	☐	☐
Amanda	☐	☐

B. Listen again. Complete the chart with information about their vacations.

Daniel's vacation		Amada's vacation	
Place		Place	
Who with		Who with	
Activities		Activities	

C. **Group work** Ask your partners about their last vacations.

Ask these questions or use your own ideas.

- Where did you spend your last vacation?
- How long was your vacation?
- Who were you with?
- What did you do?
- How was the weather?
- What would you like to do on your next vacation?
- ……

Practice and listen to Daniel and Amanda talk about their vacations.

AMANDA	Daniel! Hi! Welcome back. You were away last week, right?
DANIEL	Yeah, I was on vacation.
AMANDA	Where did you go?
DANIEL	I went to San Francisco.
AMANDA	Nice! How was it?
DANIEL	Oh, I loved it! It's a really pretty city.
AMANDA	So…. why San Francisco?
DANIEL	Oh, my sister lives there. I stayed with her. I went sightseeing, and she loves to shop, so we went shopping every day. Look, I got this sweater.
AMANDA	Nice! I didn't go anywhere on my last vacation. I didn't have enough money to go anywhere.
DANIEL	Oh, that's too bad.
AMANDA	Oh, not really. I actually enjoyed my vacation a lot. A friend from college stayed with me for a week. We just talked and watched a lot of old movies.
DANIEL	That sounds fun, too.

D. **Class Activity** Who had an interesting vacation? Tell the class who and why.

➡ ____

____

____

____

____

08 Pronunciation

A. Notice how did you is reduced in the following questions.

- Did you have a good time?
- What did you do last night?
- How did you like the movie?

B. Pair Work Practice the questions in Grammar Reference, part A again. Pay attention to the pronunciation of did you.

C. Notice how to pronounce past simple endings.

There are 3 different ways to say past simple -ed words.

/Id/ For verbs that end in /t/ or /d/ sounds	/t/ For verbs that end in /p/, /k/, /sh/ or /ch/ sounds	/d/ For most other verbs
• decided • waited • wanted • competed • started • restarted	• stopped • finished • asked • finished • looked • liked • walked • eavesdropped	• lived • called • loved • trained • scored • stayed • retired • climbed • achieved

09 Reading & More Vocabulary

Swiss mountains

Read Sophie's travel blog. She's having a great time sightseeing in Switzerland - the land of snow-capped mountains, beautiful wooden houses and delicious chocolate!

Word challenge : While you read, try to find words with these meanings. The answers are underneath the blog.

1. An informal word that means 'expensive'.
2. The style and design of buildings.
3. Visiting interesting places, as a tourist.
4. Lying in the sun, to make your skin darker.
5. Connected to art, music, literature, etc.
6. The feeling you get from being in a particular place.

I love walking in the mountains. The view across the Alps is **spectacular** as you can see! The air feels so fresh up here and the colours seem so bright, especially the green grass. It's no surprise the cows up here look so happy - but they still need to wear a huge bell around their neck so they don't get lost!

When you're out walking, don't be surprised if you meet some of the local men wearing leather shorts, called *lederhosen*, and sturdy leather boots. This is **traditional** clothing in the Alps: it's not worn to impress tourists but as a reminder of their **heritage** - and apparently they're quite comfortable too!

It can be quite cold in the mountains - so if your ideal holiday involves sunbathing by the pool, the Alps might not be the right place for you. But if you like wonderful views, a peaceful atmosphere, and long walks in a beautiful natural **environment**, this is a great **destination**."

Let's practise using some of the vocabulary from Sophie's blog.

01. It's a long flight – it's another 4 hours until we reach our _______.

(a) destination (b) heritage (c) break

02. He knows a lot about buildings. He's very interested in _______.

(a) picture-postcard (b) architecture (c) sunbathing

03. I like modern music, but I also like the old, _______ music of my country.

(a) traditional (b) low-cost (c) spectacular

04. That restaurant is very _______. Let's find a cheaper place to eat.

(a) environment (b) atmosphere (c) pricey

05. You shouldn't spend so much time _______! It's bad for your skin!

(a) cultural (b) sightseeing (c) sunbathing

10 Job Interview Small Talk

Question. 1 What time did you go to bed last night?

key expressions!

- **I go (went) to bed around (시간).**
  저는 보통 ~시경에 잠자리에 듭니다.(들었습니다.)
- **I couldn't sleep well because I was too ~.**
  너무 ~해서 잠을 잘 못 잤습니다.
- **I got a good sleep last night.**
  잘 잤습니다.
- **I slept very well last night./I had a sound sleep last night.**
  숙면 취했습니다.
- **I didn't sleep much last night.**
  잘 자지 못했습니다.
- **I was tossing and turning last night.**
  뒤척이느라 잠을 설쳤습니다.

01. I went to bed quite early because I wanted to get a good sleep for my interview but I couldn't sleep well because I was too excited.

02. I usually go to bed around 11:30 but I couldn't sleep well last night because I was a bit nervous about today's interview. But now I feel fine.

Question. 2 Did you sleep well last night? / Did you get a good night's sleep?

01. Yes, I slept very well and dreamed of traveling over the whole world last night. That's a sign of good luck, I suppose.

02. Not really, I actually woke up at 4 a.m. and went back to sleep for another hour. But now I feel fine. 4시에 깼다가 다시 한 시간 더 자려고 누웠다.

03. I was tossing and turning last night. I might feel nervous about the job interview today. 뒤척이느라 잠을 설쳤습니다.

Question. 3 What time did you get up this morning? / What time do you usually get up in the morning?

01. I got up very early because I wanted to present my best self today. So it took me some time to put on make-up and get my hair done.

02. I got up at six o'clock this morning. I live far away from here so I had to leave home early.

03. I got up around seven and did some light exercise for relaxation.

04. I got up about 5 a.m. I got up earlier than usual this morning and prepared for this interview.

Question. 4 What did your parents say to you this morning?

key expressions! - 격려의 말 전하기

- **They wished me good luck.** 제게 행운을 빌어주셨습니다.
- **They told me not to get nervous.** 긴장하지 말라고 말씀해주셨습니다.
- **They told me to think positively as usual.**
- **They encouraged me to do my best.**
- **They said "Believe in yourself and have confidence."**

01. My parents are very supportive of my dreams and wished me good luck. I think it's hard to chase a dream without valued people around me. Since my family believe in me, I could move forward. They gave me the strength I needed to push through the self-doubt and fatigue.

부모님께서는 제 꿈을 매우 지지해 주시며, 행운을 빌어주셨습니다. 주변에 이와 같은 소중한 사람들이 없다면 꿈을 이루기란 쉽지 않을 것입니다. 부모님께서 저를 믿어 주셨기 때문에 저는 앞으로 나아갈 수 있었습니다. 부모님께서는 제가 회의감이 들거나 지칠 때마다 이겨낼 수 있는 힘을 주셨습니다.

02. My parents told me not to get nervous and think positively as usual. They encouraged me to do my best. Thanks to their support, I am confident that I can make it today.

부모님께서는 평상시처럼 긴장하지 말고 긍정적으로 생각하라고 말씀해주셨고, 최선을 다하라고 격려해 주셨습니다. 부모님 응원덕분에 오늘 잘 해낼 자신이 있습니다.

03. My parents wished me good luck saying "Don't be nervous because you are great just the way you are."

부모님께서는 제게 행운을 빌어주시며 "너의 있는 그대로의 모습이 훌륭하니 너무 긴장하지 마라." 라고 말씀해 주셨습니다.

04. My parents are always best supporters of whatever I want to be. They said "Believe in yourself and have confidence."

부모님께서는 제가 되고자 하는 것이면 무엇이든지 지원해주셨습니다. 그리고 "너 자신을 믿고 자신감을 가져라."라고 말씀해주셨습니다.

Question. 5 Did you have breakfast today? / What did you have?

01. Yes, I did. I think breakfast is the most important meal during the day so I try not to skip breakfast every morning. I had a light breakfast of cereal and fruits today.

02. Yes, I have breakfast every morning. I usually eat rice and soup.

Question. 6 What did you do before you came in today?

key expressions! - 면접장 입실 전 한 일

- I went over my interview notes.
- I tried to review the questions I would be asked.
- I tried to picture what the interview would be like.
- I've anticipated questions I might get.
- I tried to concentrate on this interview process.
- I talked about the interview with other applicants.
- I tried to calm down.
- I tried to relax.

Question. 7 What time did you come in(arrive)?

01. I arrived here about an hour before my scheduled interview time. I didn't want to be late on such an important day of my life.

예정된 인터뷰시각보다 한 시간 일찍 도착했습니다. 제 인생에서 중요한 날에 늦고 싶지 않았기 때문입니다.

02. I arrived here at about 1 o'clock which is 30 mins earlier than my scheduled interview time. Since I was able to anticipate heavy traffic on the way here, I left home as early as possible to get here comfortably.

예정된 인터뷰시간보다 30분전인 1시에 도착했습니다. 집에서 이곳까지 오는 도중, 교통체증이 있을 것 같아서 여유 있게 도착하고 싶어, 집에서 최대한 일찍 출발했습니다.

Question. 8 How long did it take to get here?

key expressions! - 소요시간 및 교통수단

- **It took me about an hour to get here.**
- **It took 50 minutes.**
- **I got here by train.**
- **I came here by subway.**
- **I took an airplane from Busan.**
- **I walked here.**
- **I have searched the way to come here in advance.**
  미리 여기 오는 길을 찾아봤습니다
- **I could find this place very easily.** 매우 쉽게 이곳에 올 수 있었습니다
- **I didn't have any difficulty finding this place.** 찾는데 전혀 문제가 없었습니다
- **I found it pretty easily.** 꽤 쉽게 이곳을 찾을 수 있었습니다

01. I live in Jongro so it took me about an hour to get here today.

02. It took me almost two hours to get here. I had to take a bus and then get on a subway. It was a long way to come, but I feel great.

03. I came here by bus and it took 50 minutes. I got here earlier than I expected. So I could have time to relax.

04. I came here by subway to avoid the traffic jam and it took just an hour. I didn't have any difficulty finding this place.

11 TOEIC 동사의 시제 1

A. 현재 시제 〈동사원형〉 or 〈동사원형 + (e)s〉

현재의 상황을 나타낼 때 현재시제를 사용한다. 반복적인 행동, 상태, 일반적인 사실 또한 현재시제로 나타낸다.

We hire new staff every quarter.	
현재 시제와 함께 쓰이는 말	

B. 과거 시제 〈동사원형 + (e)d〉

과거에 일어난 일이나 과거의 상태, 상황을 표현할 때 사용한다.

Mr. Lee worked for a cafeteria in 2020 as a part-timer. The employees ate together in that restaurant.	
과거 시제와 함께 쓰이는 말	

C. 미래 시제 〈will / be going to + 동사원형〉

미래에 발생할 동작, 상태를 나타내거나 미래의 일에 대한 추측이나 의지를 표현할 때 사용한다.

There will be a special conference soon. The green bus is going to depart shortly.	
미래 시제와 함께 쓰이는 말	

D. 진행 시제

❶ 현재진행 : am / are / is + doing

► 현재시점의 진행 중인 일

► 일시적인 상황

► 가까운 미래의 일

- Mr. Robin ______________ (talk) on the phone to a client now.
- The cabin crews ______________ (greet) the passengers.

현재진행과 함께 쓰이는 말	

❷ 과거진행 : was/were + doing

► 과거 특정 시점에 진행 중이던 동작이나 사건

- They ______________ (discuss) the topic last night.
- When I went into his office, he ______________ (write) the report.

❸ 미래진행 : will be + doing

► 미래의 특정 시점에 진행 중이던 동작이나 사건

- I ______________ (stay) in Hong Kong next year.
- The technician ____________ (repair) the copy machine at 8:00 P.M. tomorrow.

01. If Anne does well in this work regarding customer service, Mr. Den _____ her to the manager position.

(a) promote (b) promotes (c) will promote (d) promoting

02. Having a healthy lifestyle can ensure that a person _____ good shape.

(a) maintain (b) maintains (c) to maintain (d) maintaining

03. While he programs the computer, Jason and Kara _____ bicycles at their shop.

(a) repair (b) repairs (c) repairing (d) repaired

04. Peter and Jason, who both know this situation, _____ the issue right now.

(a) discusses (b) is discussing (c) are discussing

05. The CQI conference _____ held this coming Saturday at Hiltan Hotel.

(a) will be (b) has been

06. Mr. Hong _____ his printing business 25 years ago in Masan.

(a) will start (b) started

07. Kotak Software, Inc., frequently _____ information technology specialists.

(a) hires (b) hiring

08. The previous system _____ users to access their banking accounts by using an entering code.

(a) allowed (b) allow (c) allows (d) allowing

09. Ms. Kang _____ from air sickness when she returned on Friday.

(a) will suffer (b) was suffering

10. Seoul citizens will _____ to elect their new mayor this time next month.

(a) voted (b) be voting

11. Because of the overbooking, some Shenco Bus passengers ______ now waiting over fifty minutes.

(a) were (b) are

UNIT 06

Accidents

• UNIT GOALS

- talk about experiences and accidents
- talk about how long they have had an object

• GRAMMAR FOCUS

- Present perfect
- Past simple

• JOB SUCCESS

- TOEIC : RC - 동사의 시제 2
- Job Interview : Work Experience

01 Warm Up Activity

Let's think about when we use these sentences.

Ouch! A bee stung me.	I cut my finger.
My ankle really hurts.	Oh, no! I hit that car.
A snake bit my finger.	I hurt my leg playing soccer.

Imagine you were in a small accident.
Complete the accident report with your information.

Accident Report	
1. Name	
2. Time	
3. Location	
4. Description of Accident	

02 Conversation & Grammar

Conversation 1

A Have you ever been in a car accident, Carlos?

B Yes, I have.

A When did it happen?

B About two years ago. I was driving and texting at the same time.

A Oh, no. That's really bad.

B I know. It was really stupid.

A How hard did you hit the other car?

B Not very hard. It was just a small accident. How about you? Have you ever been in a car accident?

A No, I haven't. I'm really careful when I drive. And I definitely don't use my phone.

B I don't either these days.

Grammar 1

A. Let's learn about the Present Perfect(Experience) with already, yet.

regular past participles
• visit → visited
• like → liked
• stop → stopped
• try → tried

irregular past participles		
• be → been	• do → done	• eat → eaten
• go → gone	• have → had	• hear → heard
• make → made	• ride → ridden	• see → seen

<table>
<tr><th colspan="3">The present perfect is formed with the verb have + the past participle.</th></tr>
<tr><td colspan="2">Have you been to jazz club?</td><td rowspan="6">I've = I have
you've = you have
he's = he has
she's = she has
it's = it has
we've = we have
they've = they have
hasn't = has not
haven't = have not</td></tr>
<tr><td>• Yes, I've been to several.</td><td>• No, I haven't been to one.</td></tr>
<tr><td colspan="2">Has Carlos visited the theme parks?</td></tr>
<tr><td>• Yes, he's visited theree or four.</td><td>• No, he hasn't visited any parks.</td></tr>
<tr><td colspan="2">Have they eaten dinner yet?</td></tr>
<tr><td>• Yes, they've already eaten.</td><td>• No, they haven't eaten yet.</td></tr>
</table>

B. How many times have you done these things in the past week? Write your answers.

cook dinner	I've cooked dinner twice last week. *OR* I haven't cooked dinner last week.
do exercise	
wash the dishes	
clean the house	
go to a restaurant	

C. Complete these conversations using the Present Perfect.

1. A ___Have___ you ___done___ much exercise this week? (do)

   B Yes, I ________ already ________ to Pilates class four times. (be)

2. A ________ you ________ any sports this month? (play)

   B No, I ________ the time. (not have)

3. A How many movies ________ you ________ to this month? (be)

   B Actually, I ________ any yet. (not see)

4. A ________ you ________ to any interesting parties recently? (be)

   B No, I ________ to any parties for quite a while. (not go)

5. A ________ you ________ any food this week? (cook)

   B Yes, I ________ already ________ dinner twice. (make)

6. A How many times ________ you ________ out to eat this week? (go)

   B I ________ at fast-food restaurants a couple of times. (eat)

D. SPEAKING EXERCISE

Complete the table with information about yourself.

And share your story with your partner.

Have you ever … ?	Yes	No
• hurt yourself playing sports • been bitten by a dog or a cat • broken a bone • stayed overnight in the hospital • sprained your ankle • had surgery		

Story Example : I have broken a bone. I broke my arm playing softball. My friend hit me with a bat. It was an accident. She didn't see me.

Conversation 2

A　Excuse me, ma'am. But have you seen a small white dog recently?

B　Yes, I have.

A　Where did you see it?

B　I saw it at the supermarket about ten minutes ago. It ran across the parking lot.

A　What did it look like?

B　It was small, and it was wearing a pink collar.

A　That's her! Which supermarket were you at?

B　I was at JK Mart. It's on Highland and 2nd Street.

A　I know where that is. Thank you so much!

B　You're welcome.

Grammar 2

A. Let's learn about the Present Perfect(Recent Actions).

have + past participle.
I'**ve** recently **visited** Rome. It was beautiful, but it was a little rainy. **Have** you **been** to the department store recently? - Yes, I have. Justin **has** recently **gottnen** a new job in sales. He's very excited. My dog **has** recently **had** surgery. But she's going to be fine. Sammy **has**n't **attended** English class recently.

B. Complete these conversations using the Present Perfect.
Then check with a partner.

1. Joan's mother ________ recently ________ a birthday. (have)
2. The Johnson's ________ a new house. (buy)
3. ________ you recently ________ to the market? (be)
4. What ________ Annie ________ ? (eat)
5. Lynn ________________ a movie recently? (not/see)
6. They ________________ Paris recently. (visit)

Conversation 3

A Jin, how long have you had your phone?

B I've only had it for a few months.

A It's nice. Is it expensive?

B It's a little expensive. I have to pay $65.00 per month for two years.

A $65.00! That's a lot. I pay $30.00 per month.

B How long have you had your phone?

A Two and a half year.

B Are you going to buy a new one?

A I'm thinking about it. But I'm looking for something cheaper than yours.

B Let's go to Tech Mart. It has lots of options.

Grammar 3

A. Let's learn about the Present Perfect with *for* and *since*.

How long **did** you **live** in Orlando?	I **lived** there **for** four years. It was a great experience.
How long **have** you **lived** in Seoul?	I**'ve lived** here **for** three years. I'm very happy here. I**'ve worked** at the hotel **since** last year. I love it there.

B. Complete these sentences with *for* or *since*. Then compare with a partner.

1. Maura was in Central America ________ a month last year.
2. I've been a college student ________ almost four years.
3. Hiroshi has been at work ________ 6:00 am.
4. I haven't gone to a party ________ a long time.

5. Sean lived in Bolivia _________ two years as a kid.
6. My parents have been on vacation _________ Monday.
7. Jennifer was engaged to Theo _________ six months.
8. Alex and Brianna have been best friend _________ high school.

C. SPEAKING EXERCISE

Ask below questions to your partner and then share your partner's story to the class.

How long have you … ?	Period of Time	etc.
• (have) your phone • (have) your current hairstyle • (study) English • (know) your best friend • (have) the bag you are using now • (be awake) be awake today		

Grammar 4 : Present Perfect vs. Simple Past

	Use the present perfect for an indefinite time in the past (과거 언젠가 : 현재완료)	**Use the simple past for a specific event in the past** (특정 과거 어느 때 : 단순과거)
Have you ever **eaten** Cuban food?	• Yes, I **have**. I**'ve had** it many times. • No, I **haven't.** I **haven't tried** it yet.	• I **ate** a lot of Cuban food when I **lived** in Miami. • No, I never **tried** it when I **lived** in Miami.
Have you ever **seen** an alligator?	• Yes, I **have**. I**'ve seen** a few alligators in my life. • No, I **haven't.** I**'ve** never **seen** one.	• I **saw** a big alligator at the new park last week. • I **didn't go** to the alligator park last week, so I **didn't see** any.

D. Complete these conversations using the Present Perfect.
Then check with a partner.

1. A ________ you ever ________ in public? (sing)
   B Yes, I ________. I ________ at a friend's birthday party.

2. A ________ you ever ________ something valuable? (lose)
   B No, I _______. But my brother _______ his cell phone on a trip once.

3. A ________ you ever ________ a traffic ticket? (get)
   B Yes, I ________. Once I ________ a ticket and had to pay $50.

4. A ________ you ever ________ a live concert? (see)
   B Yes, I ________. I ________ Adele at the stadium last year.

5. A ________ you ever ________ late for an important event? (be)
   B No, I _______. But my sister _______ two hours late for her wedding!

03 Reading

A. Read this email. Then answer the questions about the email.

To : Janine_96@hongmail.net
Date : August 3
Subject : an accident

Dear Janine,

Let me tell you about my terrible day. I woke up late, so I was in a hurry. I didn't even eat breakfast. I decided to drink my coffee in the car on my way to work. But then I spilled hot coffee on m leg. I looked down, so I didn't see the car in front of me stop. And I heit it. There was a lot of damage to our cars. He was relly angry. I told him I

haven't been in an accident before. But he didn't listen to me. He just yelled at me. I called my insurance company. The agent told me it was 100% my fault because I hit him from behind. I'm so sad. I don't know what I'm going to do. My car is damaged, and how my monthly insurance payments are going to be really expensive. And look at my car. It's ruined!

Matilda

B. Comprehension Check Questions

1. Why was Matilda in a hurry?
2. Why didn't Matilda see his car?
3. Was Matilda in the front car or the back car?
4. How do you think the man feels about the accident?
5. Whose fault was the accident?

Writing

Your Most Important Possession

Write an essay about your important possession. What is it? How long have you had it? Where did you get it? Why do you like it? It doesn't have to be expensive. It can have sentimental value, too.

➡

Group Work Make groups of three to five people. Share your essay with the group members. Complete the table with your group members' answers.

Name	Item	Why It Is Important

05 Job Interview Work Experience

Question

Can you tell me about your working experience?

업무 경험을 구체적으로 설명하는 것이 좋다. 근무기간, 담당 업무, 그 경험을 통해 배운 점 등을 상세히 설명하면서 지금까지의 경력이 앞으로의 생활에 어떻게 긍정적으로 영향을 미칠 지에 대해 이야기한다. 아르바이트라고 하더라도 비교적 장기간 의미 있는 일을 했더라면 자신 있게 앞서 말한 내용들을 언급하면 된다.

key expressions!

I used to work for ~ 저는 ~에서 근무한 적이 있습니다

- I used to work for 00 Hotel.
- I have worked before at 00 shop.

I did part-time work~ / I had a part-time job~ 저는 ~에서 아르바이트를 했습니다

- I did part-time work at a cafe.
- I did part-time work for two years.

A have taught me B A가 나에게 B를 가르쳐 주었습니다

- It has taught me the importance of paying attention to what customers need.
  그것은 나에게 고객이 원하는 것에 관심을 기울여야 하는 것의 중요성을 가르쳐 주었다
- My experiences from my part-time job have taught me how to deal with various customers in different situations.
  아르바이트 경험은 제게 다양한 상황에서 여러 고객을 어떻게 응대하는지를 가르쳐 주었다

be satisfied with ~ ~에 만족하다

- The customer was satisfied with my service. 그 고객은 제 서비스에 만족하셨습니다.
- I was so happy when I saw the customer who was satisfied with my service. 제 서비스에 만족하는 고객을 볼 때면 매우 행복했습니다.

Answer Case 1.

호텔 연회장 아르바이트, 적극적인 서비스 마인드, 적성파악

Yes, before my freshman year of college, I used to work at a banquet hall in a Hotel as a part-timer, where I could meet different kinds of people. The main customers were visitors to celebrate the wedding of a valued person and business people who had important meetings. So I needed to find out what they needed and what satisfied them first. Working with this kind of active attitude made me feel so energetic. It was then that I discovered what I truly wanted to do and enjoyed to do. Since then, I've decided to focus on expanding careers in the service field.

대학생활을 시작하기 이전에 저는 호텔에서 서비스분야에서 일을 하였는데 그 곳에서 다양한 사람들을 만날 수 있었습니다. 소중한 사람들의 결혼식에 참여하여 축하해주는 방문객들과 중요한 회의를 하는 비지니스맨들이 주된 고객이었습니다. 그래서 저는 그들이 무엇을 필요로 하는지, 무엇이 그들을 만족시키는지 먼저 알아내야 했습니다. 그런 적극적인 업무태도로 임하면서 저는 더 활력을 느낄 수 있었습니다. 그때가 바로 제가 하고 싶고 즐겁게 하고 싶은 일을 발견한 때였습니다. 그 이후로 저는 서비스 분야에서 직업을 찾고 전문가가 되고 싶다라는 생각을 했습니다.

Case 2.
판매 업무 통해 외국어 소통능력, 사람을 대하는 기술 배우게 됨

I've worked at the clothing store located in Itaewon as a part-timer. As Itaewon is a special district that foreign travelers visit often, I could speak English while working and get experience in serving international customers naturally. Working there helped me get familiar with other cultures and have the confidence to deal with different situations.

저는 이태원에 있는 옷가게에서 아르바이트를 했습니다. 이태원은 외국인 여행객들이 자주 찾는 특별한 지역이기 때문에, 일을 하면서 영어를 할 수 있었고, 자연스럽게 국제 고객들을 접대하는 경험을 쌓을 수 있었습니다. 그곳에서 일하는 것은 제가 다른 문화들과 친숙해지고 다른 상황에 대처할 수 있는 자신감을 갖는데 도움을 주었습니다.

Case 3. 커피숍 업무 통해 소통 필요성, 직업 만족도 언급

I have been working at a coffee shop as a part-timer for one year. There are many customers in the store, so all staff members are required to take care of the taste and freshness of the coffee and the cleanliness of the store. At lunchtime during peak hours, I found it more important to communicate with other employees to make the coffee drinks that I ordered quickly and accurately. The store offers many personalized drinks. So, it is essential to communicate with each other about the details on specific orders accurately, and we are doing our job well. Meeting customers' expectations and cooperating with other staff members are made me feel alive and energetic.

저는 커피숍에서 1년 동안 아르바이트로 일하고 있습니다. 매장에 방문 손님이 많아 커피의 맛과 신선도, 매장의 청결도를 전 직원이 관리해야 합니다. 피크타임인 점심시간에는 주문을 받은 각종 커피음료를 신속하고 정확하게 만들기 위해서 다른 직원들과 소통하는 것이 더욱 중요하다는 것을 알게 되었습니다. 매장에는 수많은 개인 맞춤형 음료들을 제공해드리고 있습니다. 이를 위해서 직원끼리 서로 고객 특수 주문 사항들을 정확하게 전달하는 것이 중요하고 맡은 임무를 잘 완수하고 있습니다. 다른 직원들과 협력하며 고객을 만족시키는 것이 저를 생동감 있고 활력이 넘치게 만들어 줍니다.

06 TOEIC 동사의 시제 2

완료시제는 '시점'이 아닌 '기간' 개념의 시제이다. 즉, 특정시점부터 그 이후의 어느 한 시점까지 동작이나 상태가 지속되거나 영향을 미칠 때 사용된다.

A. 현재 완료 : have / has + p.p

과거 발생한 일이 현재까지 계속되거나 영향을 미치고 있을 때

: ~했다, ~해오고 있다, ~해본 적 있다(experience, recent action)

She has learned the piano since 2012. (계속의 의미) **She has lost her bag in the shopping center. (결과의 의미)** **Have you tried Taiwanese food? (경험의 의미)**	
현재완료와 함께 쓰이는 말	for + 기간 : ~동안, recntly/lately 최근에 over[for/in] the last[past] + 기간 : 지난~동안, since ~이래로,

B. 과거 완료 : had + p.p

과거의 어떤 시점을 기준으로 그보다 더 이전 과거에 일어난 일을 나타냄

We had already had lunch before the performance started.	
과거완료와 함께 쓰이는 말	before + 주어 + 과거동사 : ~하기 전에 by the time + 주어 + 과거동사 : ~했을 때 즈음에

C. 미래 완료 : will have + p.p

과거나 현재에 시작된 일이 미래까지 계속되거나 완료되는 상황을 설명할 때 사용됨

I will have finished the work by the time you come.	
미래완료 시제와 함께 쓰이는 말	by + 시점 : ~까지 by the time + 주어 + 현재동사 : ~할 때 즈음에

01. Few customers _____ the store since it was renovated last month.

(a) visits (b) visiting (c) were visited (d) have visited

02. The engineers, who work at Qatar Airways, _______ the museum this afternoon.

(a) will visit (b) visiting (c) were visited (d) have visited

03. Emily's profit rate _____ slightly declined for the last third quarters.

(a) has (b) was

04. The two companies _____ one month ago.

(a) merged (b) will merge

05. Holy Bang health clubs _____ recently around city hall.

(a) have opened (b) will have opened

06. The employees' working efficiency _____ greatly since the new CEO joined our company.

(a) improved (b) have improved (c) has improved

UNIT 07

Sunny's job hunt

• UNIT GOALS

- talk about something they love and hate doing

• GRAMMAR FOCUS

- Gerunds and Infinitives

• JOB SUCCESS

- TOEIC : RC - To 부정사, 동명사
- Job Interview : My Strong Point

01 Warm Up Activity

Sunny - the video blogger
Help me find a job!

Meet Sunny. She's a vlogger from China. What's a vlogger? It's a video blogger, someone who makes··· video blogs! Are there famous vloggers in your country?

Sunny is looking for a job. But she's having problems finding the right job for her.

Let's have a look at her vlog. While you watch, try to catch the answers to these questions.

1. What subject did she study at university?
2. Which musical instrument does she play?
3. Which sport does she dislike?

Vocabulary

vlogger
someone who makes video blogs

career advisor (or 'careers advisor')
someone who gives help and advice to people looking for a job

juggling
throwing and catching tow or more objects (usually balls) in the air repeatedly

ukulele
a small musical instrument like a guitar with four strings

to keep fit
to stay healthy and strong by doing physical exercise

Activity 1

Put the words in the correct order to make sentences about Sunny.

1. What subject did she study at university?

at	drama	study	decided	studying	to	Sunny	university

A : ______________________________.

2. Which musical instrument does she play?

ukulele	learn	Sunny	learning	tried	to

A : ______________________________.

3. Which sport does she dislike?

swimming	really	hates	Sunny	swims

A : ______________________________.

Activity 2

A. What comes after the verb?

In her vlog, Sunny used a lot of different verbs like **try, enjoy, hate, hope** and **like**. But what came after them? How much can you remember?

I decided •	• looking everywhere
I hate •	• to be famous one day
I've tried •	• singing and performing
I enjoy •	• swimming
I hope •	• to study drama at university

B. Read the transcript and answer these questions:

- How many verbs followed by gerunds are there? (example : **tried looking**)
- How many verbs followed by infinitives are there? (example : **decided to study**)

Transcript

My name's Sunny - I'm from China.

Hi! So··· I'm looking for a job. The problem is, I don't know what to do - and I've tried looking everywhere. So··· my career advisor told me to think about what I like doing.

I love dancing··· I really, really, really like travelling. I enjoy singing and performin g··· I guess that's why I decided to study drama at university···

Keeping fit! I always try to keep fit, though I hate swimming! I suppose I just hate to be bored. I even tried to learn juggling and ukulele.

I hope to be famous one day! But for now - I need a job. What do you guys think I should do? Message me!

02 Conversation & Basic Grammar

Conversation

A I'm glad to see you, Lia. I want to give you something.

B Oh, what's that?

A They're vegetables from my garden. I have too many, and I need to give some away.

B It's beautiful! I didn't know you like gardening.

A Yeah, I love gardening. It's so much fun when I do gardening. People say I am a good gardener.

B Yeah, I agree. This fresh lettuce looks amazing.

A Thanks. And It's organic, too.

B Really? I'm going to make a big, delicious salad for dinner.

A In that case, let me give you some of these cherry tomatoes, too. They'll be great in your salad.

B Thanks a lot, Kara.

Grammar : Gerunds and Infinitives

A. Let's learn about the Gerunds and Infinitives.

Gerund : verb + -ing	Infinitive : to + verb
• **can be used after these verbs : enjoy, like, dislike, finish, avoid, mind** - Do you mind opening the widow? • **should be used when following prepositions such as before, by, of, in, and after.** - Work out before going to work. It would be great. • **can be used as subjects or objects in sentences.** - Going camping is so much fun.	• **can be used after these verbs : agree, decide, help, hope, try, learn, promise, plan, want, would like** - I would like to order some food. • **can be used after some adjectives.** - I am so happy to work with you. • **can be used as subjects or objects in sentences; however, they are not normally used as subjects.** - Jina likes to go out for lunch.

B. Complete these sentences with the correct Gerund or Infinitive. Then check with a partner.

1. James is happy ________________ her at school. (see)
2. Elliot and Sue want me ________________ them today. (call)
3. Teamwork can be achieved by ________________ together. (work)
4. I promised ________________ (do my homework) before ________________ (play) a computer game.
5. Is ________________ in a quiet town nice? (live)
6. Try not ________________ too quickly. You'll get a stomachache. (eat)

03 Grammar Focus

Some verbs, like forget, regret, remember, stop, try, can be followed by an infinitive or a gerund. The choice of gerund or infinitive depends on the meaning of the sentence.

Mary stopped eating at six. (Mary was eating, and at six o'clock, she stopped.)

Mary stopped to eat at six. (Mary was doing something, and at six o'clock she stopped what she was doing and had something to eat.)

Verb patterns: Gerunds and Infinitives

Meaning and use

- My father asked me a question. I enjoy conversation with my father.
- My father asked me to phone him. I enjoy talking with my father.

Using gerunds and infinitives correctly with verbs can be difficult because some verbs go with only the infinitive or only the gerund, and others can go with either one.

- I enjoy going to the movies. (enjoy + -ing form only)
- Jason wants to visit a museum on Friday. (want + infinitive form only)
- Tony likes eating at restaurants. Tony likes to eat at restaurants. (like + either -ing or infinitive form)

Another difficulty is that sometimes choosing the infinitive or the gerund will **change the meaning of the sentence**.

- Mary **stopped eating** at six.
  (Mary was eating, and at six o'clock, she stopped.)
- Mary **stopped to eat** at six.
  (Mary was walking home, and at six o'clock she stopped walking and went into a café to eat.)

Followed by a gerund (-ing form)

admit	advise	consider	discuss	dislike
dread	enjoy	finish	mind	practise
recommend	suggest			

Followed by an infinitive

agree	appear	choose	decide	expect
fail	hope	learn	need	refuse
seem	wait	want		

Followed by either, usually with no change in meaning

begin	continue	hate	like	love
prefer	start			

Followed by either, with a change in meaning

forget	regret	remember	stop	try

Form

Gerunds and infinitives can follow verbs in the form verb + -ing form of the verb or verb + infinitive (to + base form of the verb).

Positive

- Theresa suggested going to the park.
- Ross decided to go home instead.

Negative

The negative form is verb + not + gerund/infinitive.

- My grandparents have retired and enjoy not working.
- Frank hopes not to travel over the holidays.

Question

- What did the doctor advise taking for your cold?
- Do you need to do your laundry this weekend?

Take note : possessives

- Do you mind my going out for a while?
- I like his planning our holidays for us.

04 Activities for Accuracy

Your Name

(xxx) xxx-xxxx | your.name@gmail.com | 321 Street Name, City Name, State XXXXX

Today's Date

Hiring Manager's Name
123 Company Address
City, State Zipcode
(xxx) xxx-xxxx
hiring.manager@gmail.com

Dear [Hiring Manager's Name],

The first paragraph is where you introduce yourself to the hiring manager. Use this space to explain who you are, your professional areas of expertise, where you discovered the open position, and the reason(s) you wish to apply.

The second paragraph is where you address the specific responsibilities of the role outlined in the job description. Discuss how your work experience and job-related abilities can help you meet the company's expectations for new hires. To simplify this, try including exact words and skills listed in the job description.

- Use bullet points to highlight major professional achievements
- Remember to quantify your bullet points (use numbers)
- Cover letters that include numbers attract more interviews

In your third paragraph, look into the background of your target company and figure out how they're contributing to their particular industry. Highlight how you fit into their future plans, as well as the ways you can assist them with any goals they seem to have.

The last paragraph is where you directly ask the hiring manager to act on your letter. That's why many career coaches refer to it as the "call to action" paragraph of a cover letter. Let the hiring manager know you're excited about the opportunity to be interviewed. Provide your contact details. Mention that you'll reach out in a week if you don't hear back from them, and thank them for the time they took to read your cover letter.

Sincerely,

Your Name

Name Surname

UK address
Email and telephone numbers
Citizenship

PROFILE

Current MBA student with excellent .... (key skills relating to job application) and proven experience in ...... (as appropriate); seeking employment in ....

(Alternatively

- Key achievement
- Key achievement
- Key achievement)

EDUCATION & QUALIFICATIONS

University of Kent, Canterbury 2017 – 2018
Masters in Business Administration (predicted: distinction)

- Include specifically relevant modules and projects
- Team projects/individual projects
- Include any scholarships or bursaries awarded

Briefly include first degree and institution **year – year**

(note: If you do not wish to use the MBA as a stepping stone, begin with Employment and list your education after your SKILLS AND TRAINING

EMPLOYMENT HISTORY

Job title, most recent employment **m/yr – m/yr**
Employer, location, country

- Description of main responsibilities overall
- Description of specific tasks and achievements, using whole line space
- Description of specific tasks and achievements
- Description of specific tasks and achievements

Note: Use effective headings. If your past employment is highly related to your next choice, then consider more specific headings, i.e. Financial Management Employment, Energy Sector Experience, etc.

imj/2017

Activity 1 : Mock Interview

Interviewer **Student A**

Ask your partner to tell you about the following things. Ask follow-up questions where possible.

What I want to know is ⋯.

1. something you want(wish) to do in the future.
2. something you enjoy doing on holiday.
3. something you must remember to do this week.
4. something you like to learn to do.
5. something you love doing at the weekend.
6. something you plan on doing this year.
7. something you are thinking of doing next weekend.
8. something you try to do every day.

Interviewee **Student B**

Respond to what your partner asks you. Use a Gerund or Infinitive in each answer.

Activity 2 : It's not quite right⋯

Sunny's letter

Do you remember Sunny who was trying to find a job? Well, she's decided to apply for a job as a tour manager - someone who organises trips for tourists. She thinks it's a good chance to use her skills and meet interesting people. She's written a cover letter. It's a letter that goes with a job application to explain a bit more about who you are and why you want the job. But she made a few mistakes with gerunds and infinitives. Can you find them and correct them?

Dear Mr Smith,

My name is Sunny Zhang. I am a recent graduate in Drama and Performing Arts. I am writing to apply for the role of Tour Manager that you advertised in the Tourist Daily.

The role of a tour manager is very interesting to me. Working in the travel industry is one of the most challenging but rewarding jobs you can do. I have followed the progress of Big Fun Holiday Tours since the company was founded in 2001 and I have seen how it has continued to grow as a leader in the travel sector. I particularly like how you work with families rather than big groups of adults.

During my BA in Drama and Performing Arts I worked as a Group Leader for Theatre Workshops for Kids. I enjoy to perform on stage. It is rewarding to help children to learn to do drama. I believe that this work experience allowed me to use the knowledge I learned in my degree. After finishing my job for Theatre Workshops, I tried to learn some new skills. I learned to play the ukulele and now I practise playing at least three times a week. Therefore, I believe that I am a good fit for this job, which requires creativity and dedication. I also love to travel and visit new places. While I was travelling, I developed my interpersonal skills. I had to interact with different people to find out information and get help when I needed it. In addition to this, I also speak English and Chinese fluently. I hope learning Spanish and have recently started attending an evening course.

I have decided looking for a job that will help me develop my skills and learn new ones as well. I believe that I am a suitable candidate for this job, because I love travelling and working with a lot of different people. I hope you will give me a chance to work with you.

I am available for interview Monday to Friday from 10am to 2pm. I hope to hear from you soon.

Yours sincerely,
Sunny Zhang

05 Writing

Writing : Your covering letter

A. Let's check the below Rennan's cover letter and recognize the contents of the four paragraphs.

Rennan's covering letter

My name is Rennan, I'm a student from Brazil. I'm writing to apply for the position of Pilot as advertised.
The position seems very exciting for me. Working in the Airplane industry is a challenge. I have observed how the company has grown during the last few years and I think it is quite interesting what the organization and market strategy have done to attract people.

During my internship, I learned that teamwork, collaboration, knowledge exchange with experienced professionals will help me to develop and become more responsible.

I'm not afraid of facing problems and looking for solutions. I believe that this experience will allow me to apply the knowledge that I'm learning throughout my course. I'm determined to be fluent in the English language because it's very important for my career. Therefore, I believe that I'm a suitable person because I keep calm, work under pressure, and make fast decisions.

I have decided to look for a job where I can show my skills and grow as a professional in this area. I am available if you wish to arrange an interview.

Yours sincerely
Rennan

Did you notice Cover Letter was written in four paragraphs?

They were :

01. Introduction
02. Why she wants the job
03. Why she's a good person for the job
04. Conclusion

B. Now it's your turn to write a covering letter. Choose a job of your own - and write a 4-paragraph covering letter.

Your Name

(xxx) xxx-xxxx | your.name@gmail.com | 321 Street Name, City Name, State XXXXX

Today's Date

Hiring Manager's Name
123 Company Address
City, State Zipcode
(xxx) xxx-xxxx
hiring.manager@gmail.com

Dear [Hiring Manager's Name],

The first paragraph is where you introduce yourself to the hiring manager. Use this space to explain who you are, your professional areas of expertise, where you discovered the open position, and the reason(s) you wish to apply.

The second paragraph is where you address the specific responsibilities of the role outlined in the job description. Discuss how your work experience and job-related abilities can help you meet the company's expectations for new hires. To simplify this, try including exact words and skills listed in the job description.

- Use bullet points to highlight major professional achievements
- Remember to quantify your bullet points (use numbers)
- Cover letters that include numbers attract more interviews

In your third paragraph, look into the background of your target company and figure out how they're contributing to their particular industry. Highlight how you fit into their future plans, as well as the ways you can assist them with any goals they seem to have.

The last paragraph is where you directly ask the hiring manager to act on your letter. That's why many career coaches refer to it as the "call to action" paragraph of a cover letter. Let the hiring manager know you're excited about the opportunity to be interviewed. Provide your contact details. Mention that you'll reach out in a week if you don't hear back from them, and thank them for the time they took to read your cover letter.

Sincerely,

Your Name

06 More Vocabulary

Job suffixes

- **Job names ending in -er**

  presenter, teacher, train driver

- **Job names ending in -or**

  actor (some people say actress for female actors), translator

- **Job names ending in -ian**

  librarian, politician, optician

- **Job names ending in -ist**

  journalist, receptionist, dentist

07 Reading

Read the online newsletter about gardening.

Carol's Corner Garden

Welcome back to another week of Carol's Corner Garden. This is for gardeners living in apartments or homes with small yards. When you only have a small amount of space, you have to think carefully about what to grow. This time, I want you to consider growing herbs. Herbs like basil and thyme can add so much flavor and excitement to your cooking. And they only need small pots to grow in. In addition to making your cooking better, herbs like mint can make you feel better when you are sick. If you have a stomachache, you can make a wonderful mint tea by adding dried mint leaves to hot water. Your stomachache will go away in no time. Let me share with you my three basic tips for taking care of an herb garden:

01. *Water your herbs often after planting them. They need lots of water, especially in the first few days and weeks.*
02. *Make sure your herbs get plenty of sunlight. Put your plant boxes and pots near the window with the most sunlight. If you have a balcony, put them outside. Direct sunlight is necessary for growing healthy herbs.*
03. *Rotate your herbs. Make sure each side of your herb plant is getting regular sunlight. By rotating the pot, you can have better looking and better tasting herbs.*

Well, that's all for today's Carol's Corner Garden. Read my column next week for your weekly gardening tips. Bye!

Comprehension Check Questions

01. Why are herbs a good choice for apartment gardening?

02. Which herbs does she mention for cooking?

03. What kind of tea should you make if you have a stomachache?

04. What three tips does she give?

05. Why should gardeners rotate their herbs?

Writing Exercise

01. Write about something you love doing. Why do you love doing it?

→ *I love*

02. Write about something you hate doing. Why do you hate doing it?

→ *I hate*

03. Examples

→ I love cooking. It's fun to try cooking various dishes. I can easily find out good recipe information using the internet. And sometimes the food is delicious. When I cook for my friends, they usually offer to wash the dishes after the meal.

→ I hate cooking. It takes lots of times to make things. And then I have to wash the dishes. No thanks!

08 Job Interview My Strong Point

Question What are your strong points?

= What is your strength? / Describe your three main strengths.
/ What would your current boss describe as your three greatest assets? Why?

"자신의 장점을 이야기 해주세요."

한 지원자가 면접관에게 질문을 받고 그 답변을 통해 자신의 자질을 어필할 시간은 매우 제한적이며, 면접관들은 겨우 2~3개의 답변을 듣고 판단해야 한다. 면접관의 눈과 귀를 확 뜨이고, 시선을 붙잡을 수 있는 차별화된 답변으로 주어진 짧은 시간을 최대한 활용해야 한다. 면접관의 눈으로도 금세 판단할 수 있는 사항들(밝은 미소, 체격조건 등)을 언급하는 것 보다는, 답변을 통해 필수적인 사항(팀워크, 성실함, 적응력 등)들을 지니고 있다는 내용을 강하게 말하는 것이 좋다.

key words! - 장점을 나타내는 유용한 표현

- interpersonal skills 대인관계 기술
- decision making skills 의사결정 능력
- time management skills 시간 관리 능력
- flexibility 유연성
- coordinating skills 의견 조율 능력
- ability to adapt quickly 빠른 적응 능력
- ability to cope with crises 위기 대처 능력
- problem solving skills 문제 해결 능력
- people sills 사교 능력
- communication skills 의사소통 스킬
- adaptability 적응력
- ability to concentrate on~ ~의 집중력
- ability to handle multiple tasks 멀티태스킹
- ability to remain calm 침착함 유지

key expressions!

I am good at ~ ing 저는 ~을 잘합니다.

I have a strong~ 저는 ~이 강합니다(뛰어납니다).

- I have a strong understanding of the industry. 이 업계의 이해도가 뛰어납니다.
- I have a strong sense of responsibility. 저는 책임감이 강합니다.

I believe my biggest strength is~ 저는 ~이 가장 큰 장점이라고 믿습니다.

- I believe my biggest strength is my leadership skills in a team.
- I believe my biggest strength is that I get along well with many people.

My key strength is my ability to~ 제 가장 큰 장점은 ~하는 능력입니다.

- My key strength is my ability to stay focused. 제 가장 큰 장점은 집중하는 능력입니다.
- My key strength is my ability to adapt quickly to new circumstances.

This strong point of mine has helped me to~
제 이런 장점이 ~하도록 도움을 주었습니다.

- This strong point of mine has helped me to build a good relationship with co-workers. 제 이런 장점이 동료와 좋은 관계를 형성하도록 도움을 주었습니다.
- This strong point of mine has helped me to achieve better results. 저의 이러한 장점이 더 나은 결과를 얻을 수 있도록 도움을 주었습니다.

Answer Case 1. 팀워크

I am a team-oriented person, and I think this is very important to work with others for achieving a common goal. In the most recent team project at my university, I felt great satisfaction when I helped team members to resolve the problems. Cooperating with one another and making a good harmony with the others are very enjoyable. This strong point of mine has helped me to build a good relationship with many people.

저는 팀워크가 좋은 사람이며, 이는 다른 사람들과 함께 공동의 목표를 위해 일하는 데 매우 중요한 점이라고 생각합니다. 최근 대학에서 팀 프로젝트를 하면서 저는 동료들이 문제를 해결할 수 있도록 도움을 주었을 때 큰 만족감을 느낍니다. 함께 협력하고 사람들과 조화를 이루는 것은 매우 즐거운 일입니다. 이러한 저의 장점이 많은 사람들과 좋은 관계를 형성하도록 도움을 주었습니다.

Case 2. 공감, 이해 능력

My greatest strength is my ability to understand, and encourage people. I think listening is the first step in good communication skills and it also helps build better relationships with people. It would come from listening to others, sincerely and carefully. Among friends, I am the one whom they want to talk to. As they said, talking to me with their personal issues has helped them to feel relaxed and come up with good ideas. In addition, when I worked at my previous job, I was praised by my former manager several times for treating dissatisfied customers well with these conversational skills. I think this ability would be helpful for working as a cabin crew who should satisfy passengers and exceed their needs.

제 가장 큰 장점은 사람들을 이해하고 격려하는 능력입니다. 경청은 좋은 대화 기술의 첫 번째 단계이고 사람들과의 관계 형성에도 도움을 준다고 생각합니다. 이러한 능력은 다른 사람들의 말을 진심으로 주의 깊게 듣는데서 나온다고 생각합니다. 친구들 사이에서는 저는 항상 함께 말하고 싶은 사람으로 통합니다. 친구들은 저와 이야기만 해도 마음이 편안해지고 개인적인 걱정을 풀어줄 좋은 생각이 떠오른다고 합니다. 게다가 저는 전 직장에서 일 했을 때 불만족 고객을 이러한 대화 기술로 잘 응대하여 전 직장 매니저에게 칭찬을 받은 적이 여러 번 있습니다. 저의 이러한 능력이 앞으로 서비스 만족과 감동을 제공해야 하는 승무원으로서 업무를 하는 데 큰 도움이 될 것이라고 생각합니다.

Case 3. 항공관련과 전공자 : 실무와 지식 겸비

I am proud to combine customer satisfaction knowledge with practical experience to resolve what could be difficult situations. As an Airline Services major, I have learned how to interact with various customers to improve their satisfaction. Furthermore, taking a student internship at the Incheon International Airport gave me the benefits of seeing the practical application of classroom theory in the real working place.

나는 고객 만족 지식과 실무경험을 겸비하여 어려운 상황을 해결할 수 있다는 점에 자부심을 느낍니다. 항공 서비스 전공으로, 나는 그들의 만족도를 향상시키기 위해 다양한 고객들과 상호 작용하는 방법을 배웠습니다. 더구나 인천공항에서 학생 인턴십을 하는 것은 실제 근무지에서 강의실 이론의 실용적 응용을 보게 해준다는 점에서 저는 좋은 경험을 할 수 있었습니다.

Case 4. 협업능력

One of my greatest strengths is my ability to collaborate. I like communicating with team members who have different backgrounds and perspectives. I appreciate their diversity and try to learn as much as I can from them. In my major, I had a lot of team projects, and most work involves practical presentations. So I have divided the workload wisely with the members and shared our ideas to make the best results. I have realized that I am really enjoying working in the team and that is certainly more effective than going it alone.

제 가장 큰 장점은 협업하는 능력입니다. 저는 다양한 배경과 관점을 갖고 있는 팀원과 효율적으로 소통하는 것을 좋아합니다. 저는 그들의 다양성을 존중하고 그들에게서 최대한 많이 배우려고 노력합니다. 대학생활 중, 실습발표를 포함하고 있는 많은 팀 프로젝트를 맡아보았습니다. 그래서 팀원들과 업무를 분담하여 업무하고 또 그것들을 공유하면서 최상의 결과를 만들었습니다. 이를 통해 함께 일하는 것을 즐기는 저 스스로를 발견할 수 있었고, 협업하여 일하는 것은 혼자 하는 것보다 확실히 더욱 효과적이라는 것을 깨달았습니다.

Case 5. 긍정적인 태도

I have a positive attitude towards life. Even though the situation is complicated, maintaining a positive attitude seems to help me imagine good results and be more active in my work. Moreover, I could discover myself enjoying dealing with those situations with a sense of great accomplishment. So, I would say that I can enjoy work facing various kinds of cases with a positive mindset.

저는 매사에 긍정적인 태도를 갖고 있습니다. 상황이 힘들지라도 긍정적인 태도를 유지하면 좋은 결과를 상상하며 더 적극적으로 업무에 임할 수 있게 만들어 주는 것 같습니다. 더욱이 어려운 상황을 해결하기 위해 노력하는 과정에서 성취감을 느끼며 일을 즐기고 있는 저를 발견할 수 있었습니다. 그래서 긍정적인 마음가짐으로 여러 일을 해야 하는 업무를 즐길 수 있다고 말하고 싶습니다.

One-Point Tip **욕심 버리기**

면접관도 사람인지라 짧은 면접기간 내에 수많은 지원자들을 만나다보면 지치기 마련이다. 그런데 시간약속을 잘 지킨다, 배려심이 깊다, 타인의 말을 잘 들어준다 등 자신의 여러 장점을 나열하는 식의 답변은 설득력이 없고 기억에 남지도 않는다. 면접관이 원하는 답변은 지원자의 장점이 무엇인지, 그것이 정말 그 지원자를 나타내주는 장점인지를 답변을 통해 확인받기를 원한다. 이 답변을 듣고 면접관은 해당 지원자의 장점이 자사에 어떤 도움이 될지, 어떤 업무를 구체적으로 이행할 수 있을지 등을 판단하게 된다. 예를 들어, 내가 언급한 성격에 대해서, '아, 정말 저 사람은 책임감이 강한 사람이구나.'라고 면접관이 공감할 수 있게 만드는 것이 중요하다. 따라서 욕심을 버리고 정말 내세울 만한 장점 한 가지를 정하고, 그에 대한 구체적인 예시나 근거를 들어 이야기하여 신뢰감을 주자.

09 TOEIC To 부정사, 동명사

To 부정사의 개념 및 역할

A. 개념

동사가 형태를 바꾸어 문장 내에서 동사가 아닌 다른 품사로 쓰이는 것을 준동사라고 한다. <to + 동사원형>의 형태인 to부정사는 준동사의 한 종류로, 동사의 성질이 그대로 남아 있어 뒤에 목적어나 수식어구가 올 수 있지만 동사는 아니기 때문에 문장의 동사 자리에 올 수 없다.

- Jun-Seo wants to achieve his goal.

B. 역할

명사 "~하는 것, ~하기"	주어	To argue with everyone is not necessary. It is good to say hello to classmates.
	목적어	He needs to take a school bus.
	보어	My goal is to make the best computer programs. Mandy wants them to pay attention in her class.
형용사 "~할, ~하는"	People have the right to vote in the election.	
부사 "~하기 위해"	To book a room, he called the hotel.	

C. To 부정사만을 목적어로 가지는 동사

• refuse	• expect	• plan	• agree	• promise	• offer	+ to do ~하기를
• intend	• aim	• want	• decide	• hope	• fail	

동명사의 개념 및 역할

A. 개념

<동사원형 + -ing>의 형태인 동명사도 준동사의 한 종류로, 역시 동사의 성질이 그대로 남아 있어 뒤에 목적어나 수식어구가 올 수 있다. 하지만 문장의 동사 자리에 올 수 없다.

- Ga-eun suggests going home early.

B. 역할

동명사 이름처럼 명사 역할만 한다.

명사 "~하는 것, ~하기"	주어	Collecting Big data information is a difficult skill to learn.
	목적어	He suggested attending offline classes.
	보어	My job is playing the guitar. Mandy gave up the audience paying attention.

C. 동명사만을 목적어로 가지는 동사

• suggest • deny • quit • consider • finish • postpone • enjoy • keep • mind • give up • avoid • recommend	**+ doing ~하는 것을**

01. _____ well is an important skill that all office workers must possess.

(a) Spoken (b) Speaking

02. You can start _____ out at the park right now.

(a) worked (b) work (c) working

03. The engineer stopped _____ that robot in the factory after it was fixed.

(a) examine (b) did examine

(c) examining (d) was examining

04. _____ the tourist, that friendly local passerby used a map app.

(a) Being helped (b) To help

05. The presentation leader plans _____ the keynote speaker during the first session.

(a) to introduce (b) introducing

UNIT 08

It is helpful to get rest

UNIT GOALS

- giving advice
- requests & suggestions

GRAMMAR FOCUS

- Modal verbs
  - can and should
  - can, could, may
- Adjective/noun + infinitive

JOB SUCCESS

- TOEIC : LC - 요청문, 제안문, 평서문

01 Introduction

Common Health Problems

Check(☑) the health problems you have had recently.

☐ a headache	☐ a cough	☐ a cold	☐ the flu
☐ a stomachache	☐ a backache	☐ sore muscles	☐ insomnia

What did you do for the health problems you checked?

02 Grammar Focus

Modal verbs *can* and *should*

What **can** I do in Mexico City?	What **should** I see there?
• You **can** walk around the historic center.	• You **should** visit the National Museum.
• You **can't** miss the street food.	• You **shouldn't** miss the Unvisal Studio.

- Use can to talk about things that are possible
  : Where can I get some nice souvenirs?
- Use should to suggest things that are good to do
  : You should try the local restaurants.

A. Complete the conversation with *can, can't, should,* or *shouldn't.*

A I can't decide where to go on vacation. __________ I go to Costa Rica or Hawaii?

B You __________ definitely visit Costa Rica.

A Really? What can I see there?

B Well, San Jose is an exciting city. You __________ miss the Museo del Oro. That's the gold museum, and you __________ see beautiful animals made of gold.

A OK. What else __________ I do there?

B Well, you __________ visit the museum on Mondays. It's closed then. But you __________ definitely visit the rain forest. It's amazing!

Modal verbs *can, could,* and *may* for requests; suggestions

Can/May I help you?	What do you suggest/have for a backache?
• **Can** I have a bag of cough drops?	• You **could** try this new cream.
• **Could** I have something for a cough?	• You **should** get a heating pad.
• **May** I have a bottle of pain medicine?	• **Why don't you** try these pills?

Adjective + infinitive; noun + infinitive

What should you do for a cold?	It's **important**	**to get** some rest.
	It's sometimes **helpful**	**to drink** garlic tea.
	It's **a good idea**	**to take** some vitamin C.

B. **Requests & Suggestions** Complete the conversation with *may* or *could* to make request and *should, try,* or *suggest* to give suggestions. Then compare with a partner.

(Location : At work)

A Here's the perfect cold remedy: garlic juice, onions, and carrots. You *should* drink a cup every two hours.

B But I don't like carrots.

C Well, then I ________ an old-fashioned bowl of chicken soup! And ________ to get some rest, too.

(Location : At a drugstore)

A ________ I help you?

B Yes. ________ I have something for a cold? It's a bad one.

A Yes. I have these pills. They're a little strong. Just don't drive after you take them.

B Hmm. I drive to work. ________ I have something else?

A Well, ________ these other pills then. They won't make you sleepy.

C. Look at these health problems. Choose several pieces of good advice for each problem.

Problems	Advice
1. a backache _____	a. drink lots of liquids
2. a bad headache _____	b. get some medicine
3. a burn _____	c. go to bed and rest
4. a cough _____	d. put it under cold water
5. a fever _____	e. put a heating pad on it
6. the flu _____	f. put some cream on it
7. a sore throat _____	g. see a dentist
8. a toothache _____	h. see a doctor
	i. take some pain medicine
	j. take some vitamin C.

D. **Group work** Talk about the problems in part B and give advice. What other advice do you have?

Ex What should you do for a backache?

A It's good idea to put a heating pad on it.

B It's also important to see a doctor and …

Role Play **Can I help you?**

Student A ; You are a passenger in flight.

You need
- something for a backache
- something for a dry skin
- something for the flu
- something for sore feet
- something for an upset stomach

Ask for some suggestions.

Student B ; You are a cabin crew in flight.

A passenger needs somethings.
Make some suggestions.

03 Conversation

Dialogue 1. Airsickness

Passenger 1	Excuse me, miss, the passenger next to me seems to be having trouble.
Cabin Crew	Excuse me, sir. Are you all right?
Passenger 2	No, I don't think so. Suddenly I feel like I'm going to throw up.
Cabin Crew	Please use this airsickness bag if you need, sir. Is there anything I can do for you?
Passenger 2	Do you have any medicine for airsickness?
Cabin Crew	Yes, we do. Are you allergic to any medicine?
Passenger 2	No, I'm not.
Cabin Crew	Just a moment, please. I'll get if for you immediately. ········· Here is your medicine and a glass of water. I hope you feel better soon. **(After a while)** How are you feeling now?
Passenger 2	I feel much better now. Thank you.
Cabin Crew	I'm so glad to hear that. If there is anything I can do for you, just let me know.

Dialogue 2. Sore throat

Passenger — Excuse me. It is so dry in here and I have a sore throat. Do you have anything for that?

Cabin Crew — Oh, I'm sorry to hear that. I'm afraid we don't have that medicine but we have some medicine for a common cold. Would you like to try that?

Passenger — That would be good.

Cabin Crew — Just a moment, please. I'll get it for you shortly. ········· Here is your medicine. Please take two pills. And this is a cup of hot lemon tea with honey. **It's usually helpful to drink it for a sore throat.** I hope you get better soon.

Passenger — Thank you very much.

Cabin Crew — You are welcome. It's my pleasure, sir.

04 Language Practice

Ask your partner for advice by using the problems in the table.

Give your partner advice by using today's grammar.

	Problems
1	I really want to quit smoking, What should I do? • •
2	I want to get in shape, but I don't have much free time. What should I do? • •
3	I'm too stressed. What should I do to relax? • •
4	I can't sleep at night because I have insomnia. What should I do? • •
5	I want to date my best friend's ex. What should I do? • •

Ex **A** I really want to quit smoking. What should I do?

B If I were you, I would buy some nicotine gum.

05 TOEIC 요청문, 제안문, 평서문

요청문 / 제안문

■ 질문 유형

요청 / 부탁	Q Would you mind closing the door? 문을 좀 닫아주시겠어요? A I'm sorry, but I feel hot. 죄송하지만 제가 더워서요. **(거절)** Q Could you give me a hand? 저를 도와주시겠어요? A Of course. 물론이죠. **(수락)**
제안	Q Would you like to go out for shopping with me? 저와 쇼핑하러 나갈래요? A I'm Sorry, I'm busy now. 죄송해요. 지금은 바쁘네요. **(거절)** Q Why don't you take the school bus? 학교버스를 타는 게 어때? A That's a great idea. 좋은 생각이에요. **(수락)**

평서문

■ 질문 유형

정보 / 사실전달	Q The copy machine is out of order. 복사기가 고장났습니다. A I didn't know that. 그런 줄 몰랐어요. **(몰랐던 사실에 대한 반응)**
의견 전달	Q We need to print out more handouts. 유인물을 더 출력해야 해요. A We don't have enough time. 우리는 그럴 시간이 없어요. **(반대)**
제안 하기	Q You should use your time more efficiently. 당신은 시간을 더 효율적으로 이용해야 해요. A Thanks, I need your help. 고마워요, 도와주세요. **(수락)**
문제점 제기	Q That computer doesn't seem to work properly. 저 컴퓨터가 제대로 작동하지 않은 것 같아요. A Then I'll check the number of the repair person. 그렇다면 제가 수리하는 사람의 번호를 확인해 볼게요. **(해결책 제시)**

UNIT 09

What would you like?

• UNIT GOALS

- can choose the appropriate polite requests
- can ask polite questions

• GRAMMAR FOCUS

- Polite requests
- Modal verbs : would and will
- Embedded questions
- so, too, neither, either

• JOB SUCCESS

- Review TOEIC (Unit 1 ~ Unit 8)

01 Introduction

Popular Korean Foods to try in Korea

Korean Barbecue	Bibimbap	Fried Chicken	Dakgalbi

Galbitang	Meokgolli+Pajeon	Naengmyeon	Kimchi Mandu
	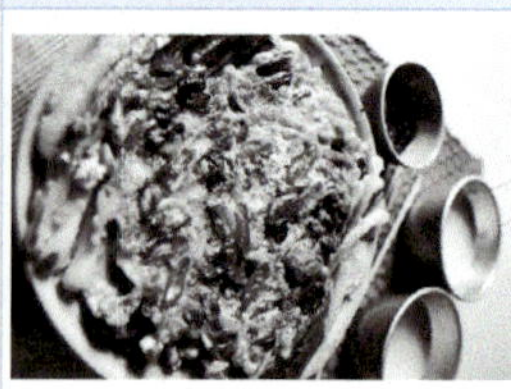		

출처 : www.google.co.kr

01. Is there any your favorite food from above? Put the foods in order from your favorite ① to your least favorite ⑧.

02. What is your comfort food? Tell us when it came to your mind.

02 Reading

출처 : www.google.co.kr

Do people around the world really eat that differently? Or are there some tried and true favorites shared by many cultures around the globe?

The countries surveyed included Australia, Brazil, Germany, Ghana, Guatemala, India, Kenya, Mexico, Pakistan, the Philippines, Russia, South Africa, Spain, Tanzania, the Netherlands, England, and the United States. Surprisingly, many of the people in these countries reported similar favorite foods.

The top three foods overall were pasta, meat, and rice. If spaghetti and meatballs is your favorite meal, you're in good company around the world! In the United States, the top three were pizza, steak, and chicken. Pakistani parents must be proud, as their favorite food was vegetables.

This study also showed that the way people eat around the world is changing rapidly. The two primary causes are increasing food prices and health concerns. In fact, over half of the people surveyed indicated that they're not eating some of the same foods they were eating just two years ago.

Q1. Among exotic food, what is your favorite one?

➡

Q2. When have you eaten it recently? Share your dining story with your partner.

➡

Q3. Read below conversation and check the today's grammar focus.

Yoon Seo	Hey, do you want to get something to eat?
Da In	Sure. I'm beginning to feel hungry.
Yoon Seo	So am I. I really could eat something.
Da In	How about pizza?
Yoon Seo	Hmm. I'm not sure. I'm not really in the mood for a pizza.
Da In	You know, neither am I.
Yoon Seo	OK. Let's look for something else. But I want to eat. Soon!
Da In	No problem. I do, too.
Yoon Seo	I like Japanese food a lot.
Da In	So do I, but… I'm just not sure that's what I want.
Yoon Seo	But Da In, I'm hungry.
Da In	So am I. But, I'm just not sure about sushi.
Yoon Seo	Where do you want to go?
Da In	Well, there's a Thai restaurant across the street. I've never had Thai food.
Yoon Seo	Neither have I. OK, let's go.

➡

03 Basic Grammar

So, too, neither, either

	Agree	Disagree
• I'**m** crazy about Italian food.	So **am** I. / I **am**, too.	Oh, I'**m** **not**.
• I **can** eat really spicy food.	So **can** I. / I **can**, too.	Really? I **can't**.
• I **like** Korean food a lot.	So **do** I. / I **do**, too.	Oh, I **don't** (like it very much).
• I'**m** **not** in the mood for Indian food.	**Neither am** I. / I'**m not either**.	Really? I am.
• I can't stand fast food.	**Neither can** I. / I **can't either**.	Oh, I love it.
• I don't like salty food.	**Neither do** I. / I **don't either**.	Oh, I like it a lot.

A. Write responses to show agreement with these statements. Then compare with a partner.

1. I'm not crazy about spicy food.

   → *Neither am I. I can't eat spicy food.*

2. I can eat any kind of food.

   →

3. I think eating spicy food helps me release my stress.

   →

4. I can't stand fast food.

   →

5. I'm not in the mood for greasy food.

➡

6. I can't eat bland food.

➡

7. I enjoy fine dining.

➡

8. I try to eat healthy food.

➡

9. I don't like bland food.

➡

10. I enjoy rich food very much.

➡

bland

delicious

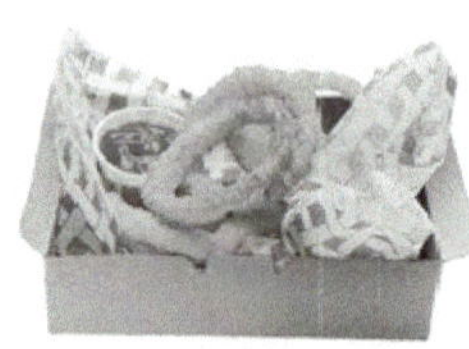
greasy

healthy

rich

salty

spicy

B. **Pair Work** Take turns responding to the statements in part A again. Give your own opinion when responding.

➡

Modal verbs *would* and *will* for requests

• What **would** you **like**?	I'**d** **like** the veggie burger. (I'**d** = I would) I'**ll** **have** a mango salad. (I'**ll** = I will)
• What kind of soup **would** you **like**?	I'**d** **like** onion soup, please. I'**ll** **have** the soup of the day.
• What **would** you **like** to drink?	I'**d** **like** a cup of coffee, please. I'**ll** **have** a large orange juice.
• **Would** you **like** anything else?	Yes, please. I'**d** **like** some sandwich, please. That's all, thank you.

➡

C. Complete this conversation. Then practice with your partner.

Server	Hello. What ________ you like to order?
Customer	I ________ have the veggie burger.
Server	________ you like salad or potato chips?
Customer	I ________ like salad, please.
Server	OK. And ________ you like anything to drink?
Customer	I ________ just have a can of coke.
Server	Would you ________ anything else?
Customer	No, that's all for now, thanks.

Role Play at a coffee shop

Student A ; You are a customer at a coffee shop. order what you want for lunch.

Student B ; you are the server. Take your customer's order.

TODAY'S LUNCH SPECIALS

Cheeseburger with onion rings
Spicy shrimp and rice
Chicken salad sandwich
Lamb curry and potatoes
Sushi plate with miso soup
Vegetarian pizza and salad

Drinks

Coffee
Tea
Soda
Fresh juice
Sparkling water

Desserts

Ice cream
Chocolate cake
Lemon pie
Fresh fruit salad

Change roles and try the role play again.

04 Grammar Focus

Conversation 1

A Have you listened to the new BTS album yet?

B Not yet. How is it?

A It's amazing. You have to download it.

B How much is the album?

A You can get it at the online music store for $9.99.

B That's not bad. But I don't know how to use the online music sore. Can you help me download it?

A Sure. Get your credit card, and I'll help you download it.

B Thanks. Here's my card.

Grammar : Polite Requests

A. Let's learn about making polite requests from imperatives.

Can / Could + you + verb (infinitive) ~ ?
• **Can you help** me? • **Could you** please **not call** here after nine o'clock? • **Could you** please **turn** the music down? • **Can you give** Andrew my phone number? • **Could you tell** Yumi to mee us at the bus stop? • **Can you** please **stop** teasing your younger sister?

B. Pair Work

01. Make a list of four more imperatives. Then change them into polite requests.

	Imperatives	Polite Requests
1	*Lend me your phone.*	*Could you lend me your phone?*
2		
3		
4		
5		

02. Role-play the polite requests with a partner.

A Could you lend me your phone?
B Sure. Here it is.

03. Choose the appropriate expression for each situation.(Some pictures will be shown in the class)

❶ Give me your phone number. vs. Could I have your phone number?
❷ Could you please turn off you cell phone? vs. Turn off your cell phone!
❸ Can I have a cup of coffee? vs. Give me a cup of coffee.
❹ Can I borrow some money? vs. Give me some money.

Conversation 2

A What are you doing?

B I'm doing a weekly podcast. I post the files on the school's website. Then, students can download the files and listen to the podcasts.

A What kind of podcast is it?

B It's a sports podcast. I discuss our school's sports teams for an hour once a week.

A Who do you discuss it with?

B I ask a different athlete to join me each week. This week, I'm talking to Antony Jackson. He's the great member in our football team. Could you tell me what time it is?

A It's 11:30. When is he coming?

B He is going to be here at 11:45.

Grammar : Embedded Questions

A. Let's learn about embedded questions.

Interrogative **when/where/what/why/how + subject + verb**	**Declarative** **if/whether/whether or not + subject + verb**
• She didn't know **when the class starts.** • Could you tell me **where the police station is**? • Ms. Kim asked me **why I was absent yesterday**. • We have no idea **how we can get there**.	• Do you know **if it's going to rain later**? • Can you tell me **whether or not Jin is coming today**? • We have no idea **if Sue and Betty live together**.

B. Fill in the blanks by using the words presented.

1. "Can you tell me ______________________ (time, the movie, what, starts)?"
2. Jake asked me whether or not ______________________ (is coming, Mia, to the party)
3. "Do you know ______________________ (summer vacation, when, begins)?
4. In math class, I encountered a difficult question. I have no idea ______________________ (how, should, solve, I , it).
5. Our teacher asked us if ______________________ (an extra day, we, needed) to prepare for the test.

➡

05 Conversation

Situation 1. At a fast food restaurant

A. Let's practice the conversation with your partner.

Cashier	Welcome to Jack's Burger! May I take your order?
Marie	We will have a spicy chicken burger with cheese and a grilled beef steak burger with fried onion please.
Cashier	What would you like to drink?
Marie	Umm··· A strawberry milkshake and a coke please.
Cashier	If you order the grilled beef steak burger and a coke as a value meal, you could enjoy it with $3 lesser. It's cheaper price.
Marie	Oh! It sounds great! We will go with the value meal.
Cashier	Dine-in or take away?
Marie	Dine-in please.
Cashier	Here you are. Enjoy your meal.
Marie	Thank you.

B. Comprehension Check Exercise

Ask and answer the questions with your partner.

1. How much money could Marie save by ordering the value meal?
2. Did Marie dine in the burger or take it away?
3. What did Marie ask the cashier for?

Situation 2. Ordering at a Restaurant

A. Let's practice the conversation with your partner.

A May I take your order now?

B Yes, um··· What would you recommend?

A Today's special is the prime rib with a glass of house wine. We serve it for $54, which is a special price only for today.

B **I'll have** today's special then.

A An excellent choice. **How would you like** your steak?

B Medium well, please. And I'd like a Caesar salad.

A All right. And would you like something to drink?

B Just mineral water, please.

B. Pattern Training

① I'll have ~ . ~으로 주세요. (음식을 주문할 때)

- the filet mignon 최상급 안심(필레미뇽)
- the seafood pasta 해물 파스타
- a glass of red wine 레드와인 한 잔

② How would you like your ~ ? ~를 어떻게 요리해 드릴까요?

- eggs
- coffee
- lamb

C. Further Expression

1. I want to order a shrimp burger with mustard sauce and a coke, please.
2. I'm sorry but there aren't any shrimp burger left. We do have the mushroom beef burger though. I would like to recommend that to you.

Situation 3. Having dinner in a plane

A. Let's practice the conversation with your partner.

Cabin Crew	Excuse me, ma'am. We are serving dinner now. We have chicken teriyaki with rice and grilled beef with black pepper sauce. What would you like to have?
Passenger	I'll have grilled beef for me and chicken teriyaki for my child.
Cabin Crew	Certainly, ma'am. Would you like to open your tray table? Here's your meal.
Passenger	Thank you.
Cabin Crew	Would you like some juice or coffee?
Passenger	Coffee for me. And for him, orange juice please.
Cabin Crew	Certainly. Here you are. I hope you enjoy your meal.

Situation 4. Hotel Room Service Expressions

How can I help you?

Hi, it's room 2105. Hi, I'd like to order room service.

What is your popular dish?

Does it come with the french fries?

Can you make the french fries well done?

What else does it come with?

I'd also want to add coffee. = I'd also like to add coffee.

Do you serve this in a jug? (carafe : jug와 비슷하게 생긴, 음료를 담는 통)

~ **We are serving in a carafe.**

How much is it in total? = What's the total?

Pleas charge it to my room.

Do we have to pay for it when we check out?

❖ 영수증도 음식과 함께 받기를 원할 때는

- Can you send the receipt with the food?
- Can you send the receipt along with the food?

* 'with' - 같이 있는 / 'along with' - 같이 함께 오(가)는

UNIT 10

What a big world!

UNIT GOALS

- can compare people and things

GRAMMAR FOCUS

- Comparative and Superlative adjectives

JOB SUCCESS

- TOEIC : LC - 의문사 의문문(Why, How) / RC - 비교급, 원급비교, 최상급

01 Introduction

The atmosphere of the cities

출처 : www.google.co.kr

02 Reading & Basic Grammar

Reading 1

출처 : www.google.co.kr

In Singapore and Korea, tipping is very rare.

But, America is the most 'tip-friendly' country on earth. People leave a tip when they pay for a meal. In New York, Leaving a tip of around 20% in restaurants is normal.

In Canada, tipping is practiced in a similar manner to the United States. Taxes in Canada are ____________ (high) in the United States. Therefore, High taxes and a Tipping manner make it feel ____________ *more* expensive.

Grammar : Comparative and Superlative Adjectives

A. Let's learn about the Comparative and Superlative Adjectives.

Comparative	the + Superlative
• Braden is **older than** Albert. • Mt. Everest is **bigger than** Mt. Hanla. • Arianna is **funnier than** Mia. • English is **more interesting than** Biology.	• Kate is **the oldest** player on the team. • Mt. Everest is **the biggest** mountain in the world. • Jeremy is **the funniest** student in our class. • BTS is **the most popular** star in the world.

B. Complete these sentences with the correct Comparative Adjectives. Then check with a partner.

1. My boyfriend is ______________ than Cloe's boyfriend. (tall)
2. Visiting Jeju island is ______________ than staying at home. (exciting)
3. He looks a little ______________ than he does in his movies. (small)
4. She's ______________ than I am. (short)

C. Complete these sentences with the correct Superlative Adjectives. Then check with a partner.

1. Who is ______________ student in this class? (tall)
2. That was the ______________ meal. The chicken was disgusting. (bad)
3. I really like Sunny. She's the ______________ among all my friends. (friendly)
4. Dubai is one of the ______________ cities in the world. (hot)

Reading 2

Read about a trip to Hollywood.

My wife Monica and I are huge movie fans. This winter, we went to Hollywood in Los Angeles, California. We wanted to see where they make movies. We stayed in a big hotel on Sunset Boulevard. It had a great swimming pool, and where were lots of restaurants and bars within walking distance of the hotel. On the first day, my wife took a picture of the Hollywood sign. The next day, we went to Hollywood Boulevard. On the sidewalk, there were all these stars with famous people's manes on them. Monica took a picture of Michael Jackson's star. On the third day, we took a tour of a movie studio. We got to see where they filmed some of our favorite movies and TV shows. On our last day, we went on a star maps tour. On this tour, a guide showed us famous people's houses. The houses were bigger than any of the houses in our city. We say Britney Spears' and Lady Gaga's houses. Britney Spears' house was the biggest. But Monica though Lady Gaga's house was more beautiful.

Comprehension Check : Answer the questions about the article.

01. Why did this couple take a trip?

02. Where did they go?

03. What did the couple do on their last day?

04. What did Monica think about Lady Gaga's house?

Small Activity

Compare College with the high school where you graduated.
Use comparative and superlative adjectives to describe your College and high school.

Ex *My 00 College and the high school where I graduated are different. This College is larger than the high school. And this College is located higher than my high school. It is quite hard to walk up here. But the school shuttle bus is very convenient, it takes a shorter time to get here by using the shuttle bus …*

➡

03 Grammar Focus

Comparisons with adjectives

• Which country is **larger**, Austrailia or Mexico? • Which country is **the largest** in the world? • Which country is **more exotic**? England or Maldives?	→ Austraila is **larger than** Mexico. → Russia is **the largest** country. → Maldives is **more exotic** country **than** England. → Maldives is **the most exotic** country in the world.

Adjective	Comparative	Superlative
• long		
• large		
• dry		
• big		
• beautiful		
• crowded		
• expensive		
• good		
• bad		

A. Write the comparative form of the adjectives.

• sunny →	• flat →	• interesting →
• hot →	• expensive →	• easy →
• healthy →	• dirty →	• good →
• famous →	• crowded →	• beautiful →

B. Complete questions with comparatives. Then ask and answer the questions.

1. Which country is ______________, Korea or Singapore? (small)
2. Which building is ______________, LOTTE World Tower or NamSan N Seoul Tower? (high)
3. Which city is ______________, Hong Kong or Cairo? (crowded)
4. Which island is ______________, Jeju Island or Dokdo? (big)
5. Which language do you think is ______________ (easy) to learn, English or your first language?
6. Which do you think is ______________ (bad) for your health, sugar or fried food?
7. Which do you think is ______________ (interesting), reading books or watching TV?
8. Which do you think is ______________ (important), friendship or money?
9. Which do you think is ______________ (good), spending time with a lot of friends or spending time with just one or two friends?
10. Which age group do you think is ______________ (happy), people under 25 or people over 50?

C. Complete questions with superlatives. Then ask answer the questions.

1. What's ______________ (good) food you've ever eaten?
2. What's ______________ (beautiful) place in Korea?
3. Who's ______________ (famous) K-pop singer?
4. What's ______________ (effective) weight loss exercises?
5. What's ______________ (good) things about school?
6. What's ______________ (bad) things about school?
7. What's ______________ (exciting) thing you've ever done?
8. When's ______________ (embarrassing) moment of your life?

04 Pronunciation

A. Listen and practice. Notice how the intonation in questions of choice drops, then rises, and then drops again.

01. Which city is more crowded, Hong Kong or Cairo?

02. Which city is the most expensive: London, Tokyo, or Moscow?

B. **Pair Work** Take turns asking these questions. Pay attention to your intonation. Then, try to answer it.

01. Which island is bigger, Dokdo or Jeju?

02. Which class is more interesting: Math, Science, or P.E?

03. Which brand of cell phone is the easiest to use: Samsung, LG, or Apple?

05 Activity

Working Holiday Fair

출처 : www.google.co.kr

A. Write the information that you know as much as possible about these cities.

Toronto	London	Sydney

Hong Kong	Singapore	Manila

B. Imagine that you are going to live and work in one of those cities for a year. Think about things you would like to know about each city before you decide which one to go to.

Ex the things you may think of could include (criteria) :

<< The reasons why you chose this city >> : standard of living, job possibilities, type of housing, things to do and see, climate, geographical location (distance from sea, mountains), family connections with a place, language etc.

C. Create a small poster about the city you research for opening Working Holiday Fair.

D. You should tell visitors about the city you researched and try to convince them that it is the best place to live.

출처 : www.naver.com

의문사 의문문 (Why, How)

A. Why 의문문

: Why 의문문은 이유를 묻기 때문에 질문 내용 이해가 필요하다. 따라서 문장의 동사를 반드시 파악해야 한다.

▪ 답변 유형 파악하기 : 응답으로 가장 적절한 것을 찾아보세요.

이유	**Q. Why were you late for the meeting?** (A) I was late due to the traffic jam. (B) I believe I did. (C) I decided to quit my job. (cf. 제안을 나타내는 why don't you + 동사원형) **Q. Why don't we leave a bit early?** (A) I already did. (B) I didn't go early. (C) That sounds good.
목적	**Q. Why is Adele leaving the company?** (A) She is moving to Hawaii. (B) She's already left home.
'모르겠다'	**Q. Why did Mr. Dan send back the CV?** (A) Well, I have no idea. (B) He's already sent it to the department.

B. How 의문문

: 의문사 How뒤에 나오는 동사, 형용사, 부사를 잘 듣고 내용을 파악해야 한다.

- 질문 유형

방법	**Q. How can we improve the quality of service?** (A) I did it by chance. (B) By airplane. (C) We need to educate our staff first.
수량	**Q. How many people visited the conference held today?** (A) About two hundreds. (B) I didn't get any replies. (C) We should do something about that.
가격	**Q. How much would that cost to repair it?** (A) We can't anticipate when he will arrive. (B) Nobody could repair it. (C) It'll be two hundred dollars.
빈도	**Q. ______________ do you go out for working out?** (A) Twice a week.
기간	**Q. ______________ have you worked here?** (A) Since 2011.

CHECK-UP

밑줄 친 부분의 우리말 뜻을 고르세요.

1. Her car broke down.
   - ☐ 고장이 났다　☐ 사고가 났다
2. How long does it take to commute from your place?
   - ☐ 출퇴근하다　☐ 여행하다
3. When you see the green building, you should turn right at the intersection.
   - ☐ 건널목　☐ 교차로
4. Let me drop you off at your house.
   - ☐ 내려주다　☐ 태우고 오다
5. Where are we heading for?
   - ☐ ~로 향해 가는　☐ ~에서 나오는
6. I made a reservation for a direct flight.
   - ☐ 직항편　☐ 경유편

실전연습

1	(A)	(B)	(C)
2	(A)	(B)	(C)
3	(A)	(B)	(C)
4	(A)	(B)	(C)
5	(A)	(B)	(C)
6	(A)	(B)	(C)
7	(A)	(B)	(C)
8	(A)	(B)	(C)
9	(A)	(B)	(C)
10	(A)	(B)	(C)

07 TOEIC RC 비교급, 원급비교, 최상급

비교급

형용사나 부사를 이용하여 둘 이상의 대상을 서로 비교한다. 비교급과 최상급의 종류와 형태를 반드시 숙지해야 한다.

■ 형태

• The actual cost will be higher than the estimate. 실제 비용은 견적보다 더 높을 것이다.
• The CEO has donated more generously than last year. CEO는 작년보다 더 후하게 기부했다.
• Recycled paper is less expensive than new paper. 재생지는 새 종이보다 덜 비싸다.

비교급 강조 부사 : 훨씬 더 ~한(하게)	• much • considerably	• even • significantly	• far	• still

• The department store was much busier than usual. 백화점은 평소보다 훨씬 더 부산했다.

원급 비교

■ 형태

• Mobile games are as popular as computer games. 모바일 게임은 컴퓨터 게임만큼 인기 있다.
• This comedy show is as entertaining as that one. 이 코미디 쇼는 저 쇼만큼 재미있다.

❖ TIP
as ~ as 사이에 들어가는 품사를 고르는 문제는 앞의 as를 없애고 문장구조를 살펴서 적절한 품사를 고르면 된다.

■ 비교급 관용 표현

• **no later than** 늦어도 ~까지	• **rather than** ~보다는 오히려
• **twice as ~ as** 두 배 더 ~한	• **as ~ as possible** 가능한 한 ~하게
• **less than** ~이하	• **more than** ~이상
• **no longer** 더 이상 ~않다	• **the 비교급~, the 비교급…** ~하면 할수록 더 … 하다
• **비교급 + than expected** 예상보다 더 ~한	

❖ **EXAMPLE**

• The nominations will be accepted no later than July 15.

• The new books sold better than expected.

01. The new presentation software is more delicate _______ the old version.

(a) than (b) with

02. Cold Blue Inc. is now _______ reliable as its competitor, Dall Security.

(a) very (b) as

03. English Speaking skill is a ______ more essential qualification for a versatile candidate than it was in the past.

(a) very (b) much

04. The newly renovated study room is as ________ as the cafeteria in the basement.

(a) space (b) spacious

05. Next week's orientation will be intended for employees who have been with the company for _______ one year.

(a) by far (b) less than

(c) no longer (d) rather than

06. MZ generation consumers responded even _______ to the new cosmetic line than expected.

(a) more favorably (b) most favorable

(c) favorably (d) favorable

최상급

■ **형태**

- Samgung is one of the oldest companies in the industry.
  삼경은 업계에서 가장 오래된 기업 중 하나이다.
- Yoon-Seo is the most experienced of all the managers.
  윤서 씨는 전체 매니저들 중 가장 경험이 많은 사람이다.
- This is the biggest change that we have ever experienced.
  이것은 우리가 이제껏 경험한 것 중에 가장 큰 변화이다.

원급	비교급	최상급
• good / well 좋은 / 잘	• better 더 좋은 / 더 잘	• best 최상의 / 가장 잘
• bad 나쁜	• worse 더 나쁜	• worst 최악의
• many / much 많은	• more 더 많은	• most 가장 많은
• little 적은	• less 더 적은	• least 가장 적은

01. The NX 2016 model from AC Autos is one of the ______ cars in the world.

(a) expensive (b) most expensive (c) more expensive

02. Yesterday's festival featured some of the ______ performances that the King Theater has ever hosted.

(a) lively (b) most lively

03. Of the three presentations that were given, the one made by the Shanti Inc. was the ________ .

(a) impression (b) most impressive

04. Among the candidates the manager has interviewed, Ms. Porwit is the ________ highly qualified.

(a) so (b) most

05. Sunnydec Resort is reviewing proposals from several landscaping businesses, and it will choose the ________ bid.

(a) most affordable (b) more affordable (c) affordably (d) affordability

06. Sorin's Lakeview Grill is the _______ restaurant that we've ever been to in the city of Swensen.

(a) large (b) larger (c) largely (d) largest

UNIT 11

What are you doing later?

• UNIT GOALS

- talk about plans
- ask questions about plans
- make and accept invitations

• GRAMMAR FOCUS

- *Be going to* and *will*

• JOB SUCCESS

- Wish Resume 작성, Pattern Training

01 How to Decline an Invitation Politely

When you're invited to a party or asked to dinner, you basically have two choices: Attend or pass on the offer. If you want to attend, the invitation is obviously welcome. But what if you can't go or just don't want to? You can, of course, decline the offer, but there's a right (and wrong) way to do it.

The wrong way to decline an invitation

"Sorry, something came up. I'll catch you next time"

"I don't know if I can do that. I'm just so swamped at work, you know?"

"I'm too busy to do that right now. I'll get to it later"

The right way to decline an invitation

01. Thank the host for the invite

"Thank you so much for asking me. It sounds like a lot of fun.", "Thank you so much for the invitation, I really appreciate it and it means a great deal."

It's important to let the host know that you appreciate the invitation, even if you are going to decline it later. Then, to bridge the relationship, ask her how the event was next time you see her.

02. Apologize for declining

You can say something like **"Sorry I can't attend"** or **"I'm afraid I'm not able to come."** These expressions work equally well in spoken or written English so you could use them on the phone or in an email.

03. Explain why you can't attend

There are lots of reasons why you might not be able to attend an event. If have already accepted another invitation to an event at the same time, you can say **"I've already got something on."** If you are in another city or country at the time of the event, you could say **"I'm not in town on that day."**

04. Offer another time to meet

If your friend asks you out for drink and you are unable to attend, you could say **"I'm afraid I can't make it on Friday. I'm available next week, though.", "Maybe another time? I'm free next week.", "Can I have a rain check?"** Don't use this for formal events, though, as it would sound rude.

02 Conversation

Conversation 1

Simon: Wow! All exams are finally over! Hey, Amy, what are you doing this evening? I was just thinking that maybe we deserve a drink or something, for doing all that hard work.

Amy: Yes, why not? We deserve it. That sounds really fun, but I can't. I'm going to have dinner with my parents.

Simon: Oh, well, maybe some other time.

Amy: Are you doing anything tomorrow? We could go then.

Simon: Tomorrow sounds fine. Maybe we could go for a bite to eat, nothing fancy, just a pizza or something ··· or maybe go to a movie.

Amy: So Simon ··· are you asking me out on a date?

Simon: Ha! No! Ha! No ··· well ··· yes, I suppose I am.

Conversation 2 : Complete the conversation.

(a) five days	(b) plane	(c) Rome	(d) aunt and uncle

Ana: Hey! No classes next week! What are you going to do?

Anthony: I'm going to visit my ① ____________.

Ana: Where do they live?

Anthony: They live in ② ____________.

Ana: Wow! That's far. How are you going to get there?

Anthony	I'm going to go by ③ ________________.
	I just bought my ticket.
Ana	How long are you going to stay?
Anthony	I'm going to stay for ④ ________________, maybe a little longer.
Ana	And what are you going to do?
Anthony	Nothing! I'm going to chill out.

Pair Work Practice the conversation again. Use the ideas below. Add your own ideas.

grandparents	Busan	train	a week
best friends	Bangkok	plane	two nights three days
→	→	→	→

→ ____

____

____

____

____

03 Pronunciation

Reduction of 'going to' & 'to'

A. Native speakers often reduce the sound of **'going to'** to 'gonna' and 'wan to' to 'wanna'. Although it is very common in spoken language, it is not recommended to use in writing. Also, the reduced form is used in an informal context, so in a formal setting, do not use 'gonna' or 'wanna'.

01. What are you going to do?
02. Is she going to be a doctor?
03. He's going to study tonight.
04. They're going to watch a DVD.

B. In conversation, **to** is often reduced to /tə/.

- What should you do for a toothache?
- It's sometimes helpful **to** take some pain medicine. And it's important **to** see a dentist.

04 Conversation & Basic Grammar

Conversation 1

A Are you going to do anything special this weekend, Alex?

B I'm going to go to the ballet with my wife.

A No way! I thought you were a sports fan!

B Well, I don't really like the ballet, but my wife loves it.

A I'm in a similar situation. I don't like sports, but by husband is a big sports fan. He is going to take me to a basketball game.

B I will trade weekends with you. I will go to the basketball game with your husband.

A And I will go to the ballet with your wife. Perfect!

Grammar : *Be going to & Will*

A. Let's learn about *be going to* and *will.*

be going to (for something you planned before)
• I am going to see a movie tomorrow. • It is going to rain this afternoon. • We are going to go hiking this weekend. • I'm not going to go out tonight. • Kate isn't goint to have a meeting tomorrow. • Sue and Marco aren't going to come to the party next Friday. • The city is going to begin construction on the new community center in 2020.
• Is the school going to close next Monday? • What are you going to do tonight?

will ① *(prediction)*
• I believe everyone will be using some form of public transportation by 2030.
• I think all tours in the future will take place in the virtual reality world.
will ② *(for something you just decided to do)*
• I'll take a break in an hour.
• The staff members will work late tonight.
• Will you have some coffee?
• What time will Grace call Megan?
• What drink will you have, sir? – I will have an espresso.
• How about this blouse, ma'am? – It's perfect. I'll take it.

B. Complete the sentences by using *be going to* or *will.*

1. She ____________ her grandparents this Christmas. (visit)
2. I ____________ her on Saturday. (call)
3. We ____________ a taxi. (take) We ____________ late. (not/be)
4. They ____________ a test tomorrow. (not/take)
5. **A** Are you ready to order, sir?

   B Yes. I ____________ the steak and potatoes. (have)
6. I ____________ from high school next month. (graduate)

05 **Exercise** One morning with Jack

Let's start with a story. A story about a businessman... an incredibly busy businessman! Have a look at the six ways of talking about the future he uses (they're in **bold**).

"Hi, I'm Jack. It's 6am and I've just got to the office. Let me tell you about the day ahead. **I'm going to** call our partner in Bangkok at 7am. Then **I'm meeting** three new clients for coffee.
After that **I plan to write** our annual report. **I aim to finish** by 5pm so that I can enjoy fantastic Friday evening! I've got to go in a minute, **I'm about to** do a video conference **with the Personnel Manager of Delhi**. Oh, that's my phone, sorry. I wonder who that is? **I'll** just answer that."

"*I'm going to* call our partner in Bangkok at 7am. Then *I'm meeting* three new clients for coffee."

Question 1. When is Horatio meeting clients?

A. Now

B. After he has spoken to the partner in Bangkok

Question 2. Why does Horatio use the present continuous when he talks about meeting clients?

A. It's a timetabled event

B. It's happening now

C. It's an arrangement

"*I'm about to* do a video conference with Delhi…"

Question 3. We use 'be about to' for…

A. Things that will happen in the near future

B. Things that have a small chance of happening

C. Things that you can only give an approximate time for

"After that I *plan to* write our annual report."

Question 4. Will Horatio definitely write the report this morning?

A. Yes

B. No

"*I'll* just answer that"

Question 5. Why does he say when his phone rings?

A. Because it's an arrangement

B. Because it's a future prediction

C. Because it's a decision he made at the time of speaking

06

Grammar Focus

Ways of talking about future

Summary

A. Will is used for statements and predictions about the future. It often expresses the future as fact - so it's used for ① very strong opinions or predictions. It can also be used for ② instant decisions made at the time of speaking.

- In 100 years' time, everyone will have an electric car.
- Sorry, I'm in a hurry. I'll take the car and you walk.

B. Be going to is used for present situations that extend into the future, or for something you want to do. There is often present evidence for the prediction.

- The government is going to raise fuel taxes.

C. The present continuous is used for arrangements. It's very similar to going to for intention.

- I'm cooking for six guests next week.

D. In addition, we can use be about to talk about that will happen in the near future.

- Quick, the film is about to start!
- We're about to leave. Get on the bus.

E. Some normal verbs also indicate plans and intentions for the future.

- I **plan** to study photography next year.
- I **aim** to be finished by 8pm.
- Mark **intends** to move to Berlin.
- We've **arranged** to meet next Monday.
- She **decided** to take the train tomorrow.

Form factor

- **Will :** subject + will + base form of verb
- **Be going to :** subject + am/are/is going to + base form of verb
- **Present continuous :** subject + am/are/is + verb-ing
- **About to :** subject + am/are/is about to + base form of verb
- **Normal verbs :** use as usual, followed by to + base form of verb

07 Activity Hit the Road

It's now time to try out all those ways of talking about the future.

Round the world trip

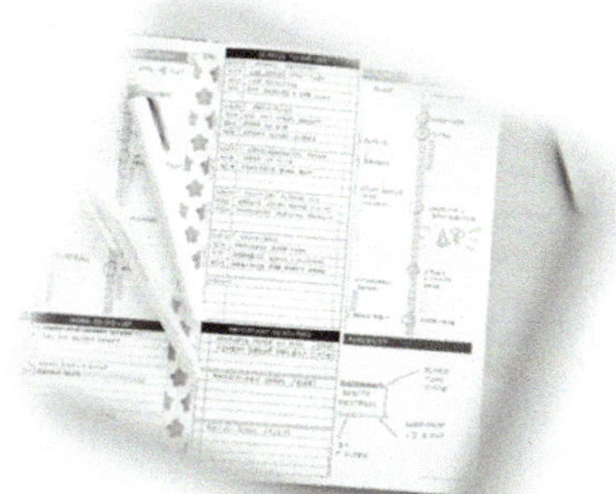

This time let's imagine a girl called Linda. She's just graduated from high school and plans to go to university, but first she wants to travel round the world. Here are a few notes from her diary :

- **Places to visit :** Japan, Australia, Chile··· maybe more
- **Where to stay :** Three weeks with the Matsumoto family in Tokyo to begin with, hotels and guesthouses in the other places
- **Itinerary :** Booked the 6am flight to Tokyo tomorrow! Volunteering in an orphanage in Thailand··· and booked a one-month Spanish language course in Santiago
- **Don't forget :** Uncle Jason is coming this afternoon to lend me his Japanese phrasebook

Read Linda's diary notes. Then make sentences.

I'm __________ (fly) Tokyo tomorrow. My uncle __________ arrive to lend me his Japanese phrasebook. My plane _________ (leave) at 6am. I _________ (stay) with a Japanese family for three weeks. Then I _________ (work) in an orphanage in Thailand. I will ___________ (learn) Spanish in Chile. I've already booked a one-month Spanish language course in Santiago.

08 Speaking Exercise

Baek, SeonSuk

18, Sangdo-ro 29-gil, Dongjackgu, Seoul, Korea
Home: +82-2-342-0345 / Cell: +82-10-3289-9456 / E-Mail: sseonbaek@gmail.com

Job Objective

Fresh and enthusiastic individual looking for a flight attendant position with 00 Airways. Eager to attain the maximum level of passenger satisfaction through utilization of dynamic personality and customer care protocols.

Education & Training

03/2014 - Present : Seoul National University of Science and Technology, Seoul, Korea
- Majoring in Civil Engineering; will earn a Bachelor Degree in Sep. 2018
- GPA : 92

01/2016 – 07/2016 : English Language Institute, University of British Columbia, Vancouver, Canada
- Finished two courses of Language School
- Studied with students from all around the world

02/2010 – 02/2013 : Sewha Girls High School, Seoul, Korea
- Earned a High school diploma

Employment History

10/2017 - 11/2017 : Assistant, Seoul National Univ. of Science and Technology, Korea
- Incorporated in operating and organizing the university entrance exam

12/2012 – 05/2013 : Staff member (Part time job), Outback steakhouse, Seoul, Korea
- Greeting customers, showing them into the seat and taking an order

Extra-curricular Activities

06/2014 – 11/2014 : Participated in Haneeum project for mobile programming

04/2014 – 08/2014 : Volunteered for a Senior welfare Center in Korea

Certification

03/2018 : Certificate of CPR & AED (Korean Red Cross)
07/2016 : Score of 865(/990) on the TOEIC (ETS)

Special Interests Traveling, Yoga, Snowboarding

References Available upon request.

I decare that the above facts given by me are true to the best of my knowedge and belief. *Seonsuk, Baek*

Wish Resume

Name : ______________

Education

- I will have ______________________________
- I will study ______________________________
- … ______________________________

Work Experience

- I will work ______________________________
- I will do/prepare… ______________________________
- … ______________________________

Overseas Experience

- ______________________________
- ______________________________

Extra-Curricular Activities

- ______________________________
- ______________________________

Special Interest (hobby)

- ______________________________
- ______________________________

09 More Conversation

Conversation 1 : Inviting and Accepting

Practice the conversation with your partner.

A Hello.

B Ying, It's Nick.

A Hey, Nick. What's up?

B Are you free on Sunday?

A Yeah. I am just going to stay home and watch TV this weekend.

B Great. I have an extra ticket for the baseball game on Sunday. Would you like to come?

A A baseball game? Sure. I'd love to.

Practice the conversation with your partner.

A Would you like to get some coffee?

B Sure. That sounds good.

A Would you like to come to my birthday party?

B I'd love to.

Conversation 2 : Declining an Invitation

Practice the conversation with your partner.

A Good work today.

B Ah, thanks. You, too.

A Do you have any plans for tonight?

B Actually, I do. I'm going to go to the movies. Would you like to come?

A I'd love to, but I can't. I'm going to have dinner with my parents.

B Oh, okay. Maybe next time.

Practice the conversation with your partner. Give excuses. You can use reasons in the box below or your own ideas.

A Would you like to go shopping tonight?

B I'd love to, but I can't. I am going to visit my parents.

A Would you like to hang out this weekend?

B I'm afraid I can't. I am going to go away for the weekend.

Possible Reasons	
• go to the movies • visit friends or family members	• go away for the weekend • study for an exam

Conversation 3 : Setting up an Appointment (formal)

Practice the conversation with your partner.

A Hello? May I speak to Mr. Thomas? This is Jane from the IC Corporation.

B Jane, Good morning? How are you doing?

A Not bad, Mr. Thomas. I'd like to set a date for our next meeting. What day would be good for you?

B How about Wednesday at around 3pm?

A Let me check my schedule first before we can make any sort of arrangement.

B Okay, I will hold.

A I'm sorry, but I can't make it that day. How about Friday instead?

B Sure. That would be fine with me. Then I'll see you on Friday.

Pattern Training Practice these pattern with you partner.

01. I'd like to ______________________. ~하고 싶습니다.

① make an appointment. 약속을 잡고

② postpone it another time 약속을 다른 때로 연기하고

③ talk to you about the appointment 약속에 관해 이야기하고

02. How about ______________________. ~가 어떠세요?

① next Monday at 2pm 다음 주 월요일 오후 2시

② Friday afternoon 금요일 오후

③ tomorrow instead 대신에 내일

Conversation 4 : Rescheduling an Appointment (formal)

Practice the conversation with your partner.

A Hello, David speaking.

B Hi, this is Jane. I know we were supposed to have a few drinks on Friday, but I'**m going to have to** cancel our appointment. Can we reschedule it?

A Sure. Jane **let me know** when you want to do it.

B How about next Monday at the same time? **What's** your schedule **like**?

A Oh, sure. Monday is fine with me. Well, see you later then.

Pattern Training Practice these pattern with you partner.

01. I'm going to have to ____________________. ~해야 합니다.

1. go on a business trip 출장을 가야
2. pass this exam. 이 시험을 통과해야

02. Let me know ____________________. ~를 알려주세요.

1. when you can make it 당신이 언제 약속이 가능한지(할 수 있을지)
2. when you can finish the report 당신이 언제 리포트를 끝낼지
3. what that is 저것이 무엇인지

03. What's ____________________ like? (상태, 외모, 성격 등)은 어떤가요?

1. your teacher 당신의 선생님
2. the weather 날씨
3. the meeting 회의

UNIT 12

Polite and diplomatic language

• UNIT GOALS

- can talk in a polite way
- can combine sentences

• GRAMMAR FOCUS

- Relative pronouns

• JOB SUCCESS

- Job interview : College Life

01 Introduction

5 Tips for Polite and Diplomatic Language

If you're too direct when you speak you can come across as aggressive and this might put people off. This is true in business meetings and negotiations, but also in many other day to day situations. Here are 5 ways you can make your English more polite, indirect and diplomatic. Follow these tips and you should make the right impression when you talk to people.

A. Listen and be understanding

If you show other people that you are listening to them, and that you understand them, they will be more willing to listen to you and accept your opinion. Don't just say "I disagree", show them that you are listening and that you understand them before you explain your opinion.

You can do this by using statements like:

- Yes, but…
- I see what you mean, but…
- I agree up to a point, but…

For example :

A I think we should wait until a better opportunity comes along.

B **Yes, but** we might not get another opportunity like this for a while.

A I think we should ask for a 20% discount because it will show them that we are serious.

B **I see what you mean, but** I think 20% might be a bit too much. It might put them off.

B. Avoid negative words - instead use positive words in a negative form

- **Don't say :** I think that's a bad idea.
- **Say :** I don't think that's such a good idea.

C. Say the magic word : Sorry

- **Sorry**, but can I just say something here
- **Sorry**, but I don't really agree
- **Sorry**, but I think that's out of the question

D. Use little words to soften your statements

- **Don't say :** I don't like it
- **Say :** I don't really like it **I'm afraid**
- **Don't say :** Can I say something?
- **Say :** Can I **just** say something **here**?
- **Don't say :** I didn't catch that
- **Say : Sorry,** I didn't **quite** catch that

E. Avoid 'finger pointing' statements with the word 'you'

- Don't say : You don't understand me.
- Say : Perhaps I'm not making myself clear.
- Don't say : You didn't explain this point.
- Say : I didn't understand this point.
- Don't say : You need to give us a better price.
- Say : We're looking for a better price.

So, those are my 5 pieces of advice for being polite and diplomatic. Try to use them when you speaking and you will become a more effective communicator in English.

02 Exercise

Practice to make our English sound more polite

You already know to say "Please", "Thank you," and "Excuse me" - but here are more ways to make your English sound more polite!

01. DON'T SAY : I WANT A HAMBURGER.

SAY ➟

"I want" sounds like a demand, as if you are commanding the other person to fulfill your desires.

02. DON'T SAY : SEND ME THE REPORT.

SAY ➟

To maintain good relationships with coworkers, it's best not to use imperatives (starting a sentence directly with a verb like "Reply to my e-mail," "Go to the bank," "Finish this project.")

03. DON'T SAY : GO AWAY. LEAVE ME ALONE.

SAY ➡

If a colleague approaches you at a bad time and you want the person to leave, use the phrases in green.

04. DON'T SAY : TELL ME WHEN YOU'RE AVAILABLE.

SAY ➡

is a nicer and more indirect way to say "tell me." It's a casual way to ask for some information. Alternatively, you could simply ask the question, "When are you available?"

05. DON'T SAY : YOU'RE WRONG.

SAY ➡ I THINK YOU MIGHT BE MISTAKEN.

OR ➡ ACTUALLY… (SAY THE CORRECT INFORMATION)

OR ➡ I'M AFRAID I DISAGREE.

06. DON'T SAY : THAT'S A BAD IDEA.

SAY ➡

07. DON'T SAY : YOUR WORK ISN'T GOOD.

SAY →

---

08. DON'T SAY : I DON'T LIKE THE COLORS IN THIS DESIGN.

SAY →

When reviewing work, avoid statements like "I don't like…" Instead, you can use a more indirect form like "I'm not too fond of…" or "I'm not a fan of…" Another option is to state what you want to see instead : "I'd prefer…" or "I'd rather…"

09. Don't say : THE PERSON WHO IS WEARING WHITE BLOUSE IS SQUEEZED BY FAT PASSENGERS.

SAY →

Relative Pronouns

Relative pronouns are connecting words that help **define** the noun it is talking about and give us more information about the noun.
Let's look at these two sentences.

The flight was cancelled. We were going to take ***it****.*

In the first sentence there is the pronoun **it**. In the sentence with the relative clause, **it** has been replaced by a relative pronoun, **that**.

The flight ***that*** *we were going to take was cancelled.*

The position of the relative pronoun is after the noun to which it refers.

Leaving out the Relative Pronoun

When the relative pronoun refers to the **object** of the verb we can leave it out.
Let's look once again at the first example :

The flight was cancelled. We were going to take ***it****.*

The pronoun **it** refers to the flight. The flight is the object of the verb **take**. In the sentence with the relative clause we can therefore leave out the relative pronoun.

The flight (that) we were going to take was cancelled.

There are different **relative pronouns** depending on whether we are talking about people, things, places, possessions or times.

who / that are used for people :

The man who came to the door was collecting for charity.

The lady (that) I saw in the shop wasn't Julia Roberts after all.

whose is used for possessives :

The dog whose collar we found lives across the street.

The man whose wallet I found gave me a reward.

that / which are used for things :

I don't like films that are really scary.

I want to see something on the news which doesn't make me sad or angry.

where is used for places :

Do the you remember the place (where) we first met?

I want to go to a place where I've never been.

when is used for times :

I can remember a time (when) there was no email or internet.

Do you think there'll be a day this summer (when) it doesn't rain?

Activity. 1

Select the appropriate words in the box to complete the sentences below.

(a) cooperative	(b) where	(c) I could expand my career
(d) when	(e) about space travel	(f) make me scary
(g) came	(h) romantic	(I) wallet
(k) a good ride and great handling		

01. I prefer working with people who are ❶ ____________.

02. I had dinner that was ❷ ____________ with my boyfriend.

03. The man who ❸ ____________ to the door is my grandfather.

04. The passenger whose ❹ ____________ I found thanked me for my sincerity.

05. I have a car which gives ❺ ____________.

06. I want to see something on the news which doesn't ❻ ____________.

07. Do you remember the place ❼ ____________ we first met?

08. I cannot imagine a time ❽ ____________ there was no Wi-Fi services.

09. I want to apply to this company where ❾ ____________ as a service provider.

10. I watched a movie which is ❿ ____________.

Activity 2.

Combine each pair of sentences. Rewrite using Relative pronouns

Ex I watched a movie. The movie is about space travel.

→ *I watched a movie which is about space travel.*

01. I met a man. He can speak English very well.

➡

02. Jack is playing soccer there. He is my brother.

➡

03. I have a friend. She knows a lot of celebrities.

➡

04. I like a person. The person can share the same hobby with me.

➡

05. I know someone. He can help you.

➡

06. This is the book. I've wanted to buy this book.

➡

07. The hotel was the Silla Hotel. We stayed at the hotel.

➡

08. I visited a beautiful city. It was in France.

➡

09. I met a person in San Francisco. She works for a famous IT company.

➡

10. I met him in Singapore. Singapore is known as a multicultural country.

➡

11. It is Singapore. I met the client last month there.

➡

12. I met a man. His name is 유재석.

➡

04 Speaking

You are looking for a new roommate for your apartment.

A. Think about your personality first.

Ex I am outgoing and sociable, so I enjoy meeting new people. I get along well with people who are both introverted and outgoing.

Yours →

Vocabulary In Use : 성격을 나타내는 단어 (장점)

Intellectual ability				
• intelligent	• bright	• clever	• sharp	• shrewd
• able	• gifted	• talented	• brainy(informal)	

Attitude towards life	
• pessimistic-optimistic	• extroverted-introverted
• tense-relaxed	• sensible, down-to-earth

Attitude towards other people			
• sociable	• easy-going	• laid-back	• honest
• trustworthy	• reliable	• sincere	• even-tempered

Positive associations				
• determined	• thrifty	• economical	• self-assured	• confident
• unconventional	• original	• frank	• open	• broad-minded
• enquiring	• generous	• innocent	• ambitious	• assertive

* p.30, '성격을 나타내는 단어(장점)' 참조

B. Think about what characteristics are important in a roommate to live with.

Ex I am looking for a roommate who is similar in age. I would like to find a roommate who is organized and clean. It is important that she is friendly person.

Yours ➡ ____

____

____

C. Compare your thoughts with your partner.

Ex

You	What is important to you in a roommate?
Your Partner	I want a roommate who is fun. How about you?
You	I would like a roommate who is organized and clean.

05 Practice More

A. Choose the correct relative pronoun for each sentence.

01. Elton John is the singer (which / when / who) sang Tiny Dancer.

02. That's the café (which / where / who) I met my husband.

03. I like books (where / who / which) have strong main characters.

04. The person (when / who / which) I miss the most is my best friend.

05. Italy is the country (who / when / where) the renaissance began.

06. Summer is a time (where / who / when) people go travelling.

07. There's a restaurant in the city center (which / where / who) you can eat paella.

08. The car (who / which / where) has a scratch on the side is mine.

B. Rewrite the sentences, combining them together.

01. The last time I saw my best friend was at a festival. She is from Australia.

➡

02. Have you watched that film yet? I recommended it to you last month.

➡

03. I've never met that woman. My cousin is talking to her.

➡

04. I want to buy that handbag. It has grey buttons.

➡

05. I'll never forget that moment. I met my boyfriend that time.

➡

06. This is the playground. We used to play there every day as children.

➡

07. That's the window. It was broken last week.

➡

06 Job Interview College Life

Can you tell me about your college life?

= What was the most impressive thing in your college life?

= Describe your most rewarding college experience?

Please~!!!

- 동아리 내에서 맡은 역할 언급, 경험과 힘들었던 점, 극복 사례
- 봉사활동
- 교환학생이나 기타 프로그램 참여
- 다양한 아르바이트 경험

위의 내용과 같이 학과 공부 이외의 학교 활동에 대해서 답변하면 됩니다.

key expressions! - 대학생활 관련

- I was able to obtain a scholarship. 장학금을 받을 수 있었습니다.
- It was a rewarding(useful) experience. 보람 있는(유익한) 경험이었습니다.
- I never neglected my studies. 결코 학업을 게을리 하지 않았습니다.
- I enjoyed myself immensely when I was in college. 대학생활을 무척 즐겼습니다.

Pattern **I participated in ~. (took part in/was involved in)** 저는 ~에 참여했었습니다.

- I participated in an internship program. 인턴쉽 프로그램에
- I participated in every school event. 모든 학교 행사에
- I participated in many extracurricular activities. 다양한 학과 외 활동에

Pattern **I learned how to ~.** 저는 ~하는 법을 배웠습니다.

- I learned how to deal with unexpected situations.
  예기치 못한 상황에 대처하는 법을 배웠습니다.
- I learned how to get along well with different people.
  다양한 사람들과 어울리는 법을 배웠습니다.
- I learned how to work as a team. 팀으로 일하는 법을 배웠습니다.

Answer Case 1. 친구와 함께 자취하며 학교행사 참여

My college is located in 00. As the college was far from my house, I rented a room nearby and stayed with my friends. We spent a lot of time together and shared our thoughts and joyous moments together. Most of all, we worked very hard to achieve our goals. We tried to participate in every school event to gain various experiences. I feel that I cherished every moment of my college life.

제 대학은 00에 위치해 있습니다. 학교가 제 집과는 멀어서, 저는 방을 얻어서 친구들과 함께 살았습니다. 저희들은 많은 시간을 함께 보내고, 서로의 생각을 공유하며 즐거운 순간들을 함께 보냈습니다. 무엇보다도 저희들은 저희들의 목표를 이루기 위해 열심히 노력했습니다. 또한 다양한 경험을 쌓기 위해 모든 학교 행사에 참가하려고 하였습니다. 저는 제 대학생활의 모든 순간을 소중하게 생각합니다.

Case 2. 학생회 활동-학교행사 운영

There were various events throughout the year such as academic fairs, sports events, school trips, and so on. As a member of the students' association I planned and managed events with my classmates, professors, and college staff. Through those experiences I learned how to deal with unexpected situations and what qualities are required to be a good team player.

대학시절 학교축제와 체육행사, 수학여행 등 다양한 행사가 연중 있었습니다. 학생회의 일원으로서, 친구들과 교수님들, 그리고 학교 직원들과 함께 행사를 계획하고 운영하였습니다. 이러한 경험을 통해 예기치 못한 상황에 대처하는 방법을 배웠고 또한 좋은 팀원이 되기 위해 필요한 자질이 무엇인지에 대해 배울 수 있었습니다.

Case 3. 스피치 대회 참여, 자신감

The most impressive thing in my college life was that I took part in a speech contest. Preparing for the contest was very difficult. I made a substantial effort and it gave me the opportunity to learn a lot and I gained confidence to speak in front of people.

대학시절 가장 보람이 있었던 경험은 스피치 대회에 참여했던 것입니다. 대회를 준비하는 것은 상당히 힘들었습니다. 저는 많은 노력을 쏟았고, 많은 것을 배울 수 있는 기회를 얻었습니다. 그리고 사람들 앞에서 말을 하는데 자신감을 갖게 되었습니다.

Case 4. 해외 연수 경험

The most memorable moment for me was when I got the opportunity to study in England with the support of my college. Students above a certain TOEIC score were eligible for the opportunity. I studied very hard in order to do well on the TOEIC test. I really enjoyed my life in England. I improved my English a lot and experienced a variety of things in England.

가장 기억에 남는 순간은 제가 학교의 지원으로 영국에서 공부할 기회를 갖게 되었을 때입니다. 일정 점수 이상의 토익점수를 받은 학생들이 그 기회를 얻을 수 있었습니다. 저는 토익 시험을 잘 보기 위해 열심히 공부했었습니다. 영국에서의 생활은 매우 즐거웠습니다. 영어 실력을 상당히 향상시킬 수 있었고, 영국에서 다양한 경험을 하였습니다.

Case 5. 학교-댄스동아리

I participated in a dance club during my college years as I liked dancing since middle school. We, the dance club, performed in every school event and practiced the dance performance really hard for several months. Though preparing for this physical performance was sometimes challenging, every moment when we gathered was so fun and enthusiastic. With these efforts and passionate spirit, we made nice performances cheering on one another.

대학에 다니는 동안 중학생 때부터 저는 춤추는 것을 좋아했기 때문에 교내 댄스 동아리에서 활동했습니다. 댄스 동아리인 저희들은 모든 학교 행사에서 공연을 펼쳤고, 몇 달씩 정말 열심히 공연을 연습했습니다. 육체적은 공연을 연습하는 것이 가끔은 힘들기도 하였지만 멤버들이 모일 때마다 항상 재미있었고 열정들이 넘쳤습니다. 이러한 노력과 열정으로 저희는 서로를 응원하며 멋진 공연을 펼칠 수 있었습니다.

Case 6. 학생위원회 학교대표로 행사진행

I was a member of the student committee which organized and prepared for various school events. I majored in airline service so the task of guiding VIP guests to the venue was given to me. I always kept in mind that I was the representative of my school and this naturally led me to have a strong sense of responsibility. Serving VIP guests required me to be very careful with my behavior. Due to this, I developed excellent manners and courteous behavior.

저는 다양한 학교 행사를 준비하고 운영하는 학생위원회의 일원이었습니다. 저는 항공서비스를 전공했습니다. 그래서 귀빈들을 행사장으로 안내하는 일이 제게 주어졌습니다. 따라서 늘 제가 학교를 대표하는 사람이라는 것을 마음에 새겼고, 이는 자연스럽게 제 일에 대한 강한 책임감을 갖도록 이끌었습니다. 귀빈을 모신다는 것은 제가 모든 행동을 신중하게 하도록 만들었습니다. 이 때문에 저는 훌륭한 매너와 예의 바른 행동을 갖추게 되었습니다.

Reference

- 5 tips for polite and diplomatic language. (n.d.). Retrieved February 15, 2023, from https://www.londonschool.com/blog/5-tips-polite-and-diplomatic-language/
- Course: Intermediate / unit 17 / Session 1 / activity 3. (2023, February 14). Retrieved February 15, 2023, from https://www.bbc.co.uk/learningenglish/english/course/intermediate/unit-17/session-1/activity-3
- Dubbini, J. (2019, December 10). Looking for a job - sunny the vlogger. Retrieved February 15, 2023, from https://www.englishpiecebypiece.com/looking-for-a-job-sunny-the-vlogger/
- English, V. (2017, December 29). Learn prefixes, suffixes to expand your vocabulary. Retrieved February 15, 2023, from https://learningenglish.voanews.com/a/learn-prefixes-and-suffixes-to-expand-your-vocabulary/4140658.html
- Get to know the neighbours. (n.d.). Retrieved February 15, 2023, from https://www.teachingenglish.org.uk/teaching-resources/teaching-adults/lesson-plans/pre-intermediate-a2/get-know-neighbours
- Han, Y., Jeong, H., & Kim, E. (2019). Tomato TOEIC Saenggicho. Seoul: NE Neungnyul.
- Ma, G. (2019). How to crack the cabin crew job interview. Seoul: Hanol Publishing Company.
- McBain, J. (2017). People and Life1.Darakwon Publishing Company.
- McBain, J. (2017). People and Life2.Darakwon Publishing Company.
- Present continuous games worksheets ESL activities - teach-this.com. (n.d.). Retrieved February 14, 2023, from https://www.teach-this.com/grammar-activities-worksheets/present-continuous
- Probability. (n.d.). Retrieved February 15, 2023, from https://learnenglish.britishcouncil.org/grammar/english-grammar-reference/probability
- Richards, J. C., Hull, J., & Proctor, S. (2017). Interchange. Cambridge: Cambridge University Press.
- Sethi, R. (n.d.). How to decline an invitation without being a jerk. Retrieved February 15, 2023, from https://www.businessinsider.com/how-to-decline-an-invitation-without-being-a-jerk-2016-12
- Superlatives. (n.d.). Retrieved February 15, 2023, from https://www.teach-this.com/grammar-activities-worksheets/superlatives

Answer Key

UNIT 01 Greeting and salutations

❷ Warm Up Activity

A

intimate ②, Etiquette ②, Fed up ①, Politeness ①

B

01. Informal, 02. Formal, 03. Informal, 04. Formal,
05. Informal 06. Formal, 07. Informal, 08. Formal

❹ Basic Grammar

What, Where, Why, When, Who

❻ Grammar Focus

1. Yes, I am hungry.
   No, I missed the bus.
2. I didn't have breakfast.
   I got here about 30 minutes ago.
1. Are you playing football tomorrow?
   Was the weather nice yesterday?
   Can Jenny speak Chinese?
   Did you go to the cinema on Saturday?
2. Who wants ice cream for dessert?
   Who broke the mirror in the dining room?
   Who answered the phone?
   Where did you go at the weekend?
   Where does your brother work?
   Who will you ask for help?

Take Note

big/old/much

Comprehension Check Exercise

1. Did you go anywhere interesting last weekend?
2. Where did you grow up?
3. How much did you pay for your new car?
4. When did you move into your new house?
5. What are you listening to?
6. Who won the basketball game?
7. Can I borrow your phone?
8. Do you want to watch a movie tonight?

❼ Activity

C-a.

1. **shy,** 2. **serious,** 3. **sociable,** 4. **kind,** 5. **confident,**
6. **generous,** 7. **humorous,** 8. **reliable**

❽ TOEIC 문장의 구성요소

A. 주어
The man/They/Using it

B. 동사

is/goes/will make

C. 목적어

a letter/the reply/us/to/-ing

D. 보어

1. counseling specialist/kind
2. captain/intelligent

01. b, 02. b, 03. a, 04. a, 05. b

UNIT 02 What's she like?

❶ Introduction

Q1. She is very cheerful and friendly. She is so warm-hearted.
Q2. She likes to try out famous restaurants and have tasty food.

❸ Basic Grammar

Comprehension Check Exercise

(1) What does he look like?
(2) What's the weather like?
(3) What do they look like?

Describing people

A

How old is your brother?
How tall are you?
What color is her hair?
Does he wear glasses?
What does he look like?
How long is your sister's hair?

Modifiers with present participles and prepositions

A

2. Mark and Eve are the middle-aged couple talking to Michael.
3. Alexis is the young girl in a white T-shirt and blue jeans.
4. Iris is the woman in the green dress sitting to the left of Mandy.
5. Mac is the serious-looking man playing a chess.

❽ TOEIC 문장의 5형식

A

He dances.
He goes to Seoul.
She smiles beautifully.
Jackson goes to work by bus.

B

The new product is attractive.
Kim will be a doctor.
He looks scared.
It is a good idea.

C

나는 방에 가고 싶다.
그는 책 읽는 것을 좋아한다.

D

He gave me a shirt.(He gave a shirt to me.)
I will buy you an ice cream.(I will buy an ice cream to you.)
Nick made his son a toy house.

E

He names him Sam.
그 냄새는 모두를 배고프게 하였다.
He leaves her do her work.
Leave the door open, please.
01. (b), 02. (b), 03. (b), 04. (b), 05. (a)

UNIT 03 I like to stay in shape

❶ Introduction

Q1. (an example answer) Yes, I do. I go bike riding every weekend.
Q2. do stretching, play basketball, go jogging, play soccer, do weight lifting, play volleyball, go bike riding, play golf, do martial arts, do Pilates, go swimming, do yoga

❷ Build Up1

(ex) I wake up at 7:30 every morning.

I put on make up after washing up.
I go to school by bus at 10:00.

❹ Basic Grammar

Complete sentences

1. doesn't have, 2. went, 3. traveled, 4. exercise
5. brushes, 6. didn't see, 7. practice, 8. do, go

❺ Grammar Focus

Comprehension Check Exercise

B. Pair Work
Do you ever play sports?
Sure. I play soccer twice a week.
2. What do you usually do on Saturday morning?
Nothing much. I almost always sleep until noon.
3. Do you often lift weights at the gym?
No, I hardly ever lift weights.
4. Do you always exercise on Sundays?
No, I never exercise on Sundays.
5. What do you usually do after class?
I go out with my classmates about three times a week.
6. Do you often go to the movies?
Yes, I go to the movies once a week.
7. Do you ever go bike riding?
No, I hardly ever ride a bike.
8. Do you sometimes walk to school?
Sure, I walk to school five days a week.

Comprehension Check Exercise

How good are you
How long do you
How often do you
How well do you

❽ TOEIC 형용사/부사

형용사의 형태와 역할

A. 형용사의 개념 및 형태
명사의 성질이나 상태를 표현
Ex) helpful advice, the problem is serious.
B. 형용사의 역할
명사 수식, 주격 목적격보어
C. <be+형용사+전치사> 구문
Be aware of~을 잘 알다
Be confident in ~에 자신이 있다
Befamiliar with ~에 익숙하다
Beresponsible for ~에 책임이 있다
Beavailable for ~이 이용 가능하다
Beconcerned about ~에 대해 걱정하다

부사의 형태와 역할

A. 부사의 개념 및 형태
'어떻게'에 해당되는 방법이나 정도를 설명해 주는 말
주로 <형용사+ly>의 형태 : highly, finally, quickly, generally, actually, immediately, etc. (그 외의 형태: very, too, well, still also, quite 등)
B. 부사의 역할
동사, 형용사, 부사, 문장 전체를 수식하는 역할
위치: 수식해주는 부분 앞
C. 기타 중요 부사
빈도부사: always, usually, often, frequently …
시간부사: once, ago, recently, lately, now …
강조부사: just, only, even
(참고) 동사구속 부사 자리
: 조동사, be동사, have동사와 함께 쓰일 때는 동사구사이 위치
We must completely finish the report by tomorrow.
The missing book was quickly reㄴplaced with a new copy.
Our expenses have significantly decreased.
01. (a), 02. (a), 03. (a), 04. (a), 05. (b)

UNIT 04 What to wear

❶ Introduction

I just play it safe

[teacher's dialogue]
My name is Mandy. I work in this university.
I'm wearing a dark blue suit with a white shirt and black shoes.
I normally wear formal suits for work.
But at the weekends I wear different clothes. I like comfy style. I usually wear hooded shirt, jeans with shirts. My favorite fashion item is the hooded shirt. You can pair it with anything. It's really comfy.
When I need to dress up a little bit, I just wear black and white. I don't normally wear anything with vivid or loud colors. When it comes to fashion, I just play it safe.
01. A : She works in university.
02. A : She normally wears formal suits for work.
03. A : She is wearing a dark blue suit (now).
04. A : She wears hooded shirt, jeans with shirts.
05. A : Her favorite fashion item is the hooded shirt. Because she thinks she can pair it with anything, and it's really comfy.

❷ Build Up

Answer the following questions to build up the sentence.

A. I don't know.
B. I don't know.
C. 'is' and 'ing'
D. she/She is wearing a dark blue suit now.
E. (students' answers)
F. she/(긍정: Yes, she is wearing a gold ring now.)
(부정: No, she is not a gold ring now.)

Exercise

(Session Vocabulary)

* hoodie/hoody - casual clothing for the top part of your body, usually made of cotton, with a hood to cover your head
* jumper- warm clothing for the top part of your body, usually made of wool
* trainers- comfortable sports shoes
* smart casual- describes clothes that are a mix of smart and casual, for example, nice jeans and a shirt
* graphic designer- someone who designs pictures and text for things like websites, magazines and posters
* branding- giving a company a particular look, feel or design to help it sell its products or services

(Questions)

A. Ed is wearing grey trainers.
B. She wears smart casual.
C. Charlotte says she is wearing scruffy clothes.
D. It's Ed. He is a graphic designer.

❹ Conversation

Vocabulary :

B. (1) fever, (2) headache, (3) sore throat, (4) cold or flue

❺ Basic Grammar

PAIR ACTIVITY : Present Continuous Party

(ex) Name: Mandy
Your job: I am a DJ.
What are you doing at the party?
I am playing music.
Are you enjoying the party?
Yes, I am having a fun time. Because it has been so long time to get together with my friends here.

❻ Grammar Focus

Comprehension Check Exercise

1. Does it snow in the UK? (h) Only in winter.
→ Use the present simple for truths and facts.
2. Is it snowing in the UK? (g) Not right now.
→ Use the present continuous for things that are/aren't happening now.
3. Do you work here? (b) Yes, I'm the managing director.
→ Use the present simple for permanent situations.

4. Are you working today? (c) No, I've got a day off.
→ Use the present continuous for temporary situations.
5. Where do you live? (a) My home's in Brazil.
→ Use the present simple for permanent situations.
6. Where are you living? (f) In a friend's flat in London.
→ Use the present continuous for temporary situations.
7. What do you drink? (d) Usually just coke.
→ Use the present simple for habits.
8. What are you drinking? (e) It's water.
→ Use the present continuous for things happening now.

❽ TOEIC 사진묘사

A.

(1) is serving, (2) is being served, (3) are holding
(4) is being cooked, (5) is taking

B.

(1) are looking, (2) is typing, (3) is holding
(4) is wearing, (5) are standing

UNIT 05 What did you do last weekend?

❷ Warm Up Activity

A.

do - chores, the laundry
go - sightseeing, fishing, dancing, camping, shopping
have - a good time, a lot of fun
make - the bed, a video
take - a bike riding, a trip

❹ Basic Grammar

Comprehension Check Exercise 1

A.
(1) Did / stay / called / drove
(2) did / spend / had / enjoyed / didn't like
(3) did / do / saw / loved
(4) Did / do / did / went / spent
(5) Did / go / didn't / invited / cooked

Comprehension Check Exercise 2

(1) Were / wasn't / was / was / was / was
(2) were / were / Were / weren't
(3) Were / was / were / was

❺ Speaking Exercise

(Question) What did you do last weekend?

When I woke up in the morning, the sun was shining, and the birds were singing. So, I went to the park near my place to take a walk with my daughter. While we were walking along the Han River, I suddenly felt hungry. So we dropped by the café. People were laughing and chatting. We sat down and ordered some drinks and light food. Everything was perfect. I guess my daughter felt happy. On the way back home, she was constantly singing.

❻ Grammar Focus

Comprehension Check Exercise

(1) were you doing / called
(2) was sitting / called
(3) arrived / was(were)
(4) was watching / heard
(5) went / had / met
(6) were playing / hurt
(7) were they doing / was
(8) was taking / rang
(9) was / rang
(10) walked / was working
(11) as / as shining / were singing / was walking / met
(12) was living / started
(13) got / were waiting
(14) was / was always leaving
(15) visited / saw / spent
(16) were you standing / came
(17) lived / were
(18) were listening
(19) left / was snowing
(20) was working / met

❼ Listening

I was on vacation

A. Daniel : Yes / Amanda : Yes
B. Daniel's vacation
Place : San Francisco
Who with : sister
Activities : went sightseeing, went shopping
Amanda's vacation
Place : home
Who with : a friend from college
Activities : talked, watched movies

❾ Reading & More Vocabulary

Word challenge

(1) pricey, (2) architecture, (3) sightseeing,
(4) sunbathing, (5) cultural, (6) atmosphere

Let's practise using some of the vocabulary from Sophie's blog.

(1) a, (2) b, (3) a, (4) c, (5) c

⓫ TOEIC 동사의 시제 1

A. 현재시제와 함께 쓰이는 말

usually(보통), often(자주), always(항상), now(지금), these days(요즘에는), every[each]+시간명사(매~, ~마다)

B. 과거 시제와 함께 쓰이는 말

yesterday, then(그때), once(한번은), last+때(지난~), in+과거연도(~에), 시간 표현(a week, two years 등)+ago(~전에)

C. 미래 시제와 함께 쓰이는 말

tomorrow(내일), soon(곧), shortly(곧), next+때(다음~), in the near future(가까운 시일 내에)

D. 현재진행과 함께 쓰이는 말

at the moment, today, this week …, now, soon, later today, etc.
01. c, 02. b, 03. a, 04. c, 05. a, 06. b, 07. a,
08. c, 09. b, 10. b, 11. b

UNIT 06 Accidents

❶ Warm Up Activity

(the accident report example)

Name : Yoon
Time : last summer vacation
Location : in Kuala Lumpur, Malaysia
Description of Accident : the left collarbone was fractured.

❷ Conversation & Grammar

Conversation 1

C. Complete these conversation using the Present Perfect.

(1) have / been
(2) Have / played / haven't
(3) have / been / haven't seen
(4) Have / been / haven't gone
(5) Have / cooked / have / made
(6) Have / gone / have eaten

Conversation 2

B. Complete these conversation using the Present Perfect.

(1) has / had
(2) has bought
(3) Have / been

(4) has / eaten
(5) has not seen (hasn't seen)
(6) have visited

Conversation 3

B. Complete these conversation with for and since.

(1) for, (2) for, (3) since, (4) for, (5) for,
(6) since, (7) for, (8) since

D. Complete these conversation using the Present Perfect.

(1) Have / sung / did / sang
(2) Have / lost / haven't / has lost
(3) Have / gotten / have / have gotten
(4) Have / seen / did / saw
(5) Have / been / didn't / was

❻ TOEIC 동사의 시제 2

01. d, 02. a, 03. a, 04. a, 05. a, 06. c

UNIT 07 Sunny's job hunt

❶ Warm Up Activity

Activity 1

(1) Sunny decided to study drama at university.
(2) Sunny tried to learn ukulele.
(3) Sunny really hates swimming.

Activity 2

I decided to study drama at university.
I hate swimming.
I've tried looking everywhere.
I enjoy singing and performing.
I hope to be famous one day.

❷ Conversation & Basic Grammar

Grammar

B. Complete these sentences with the correct gerund or infinitive.

(1) to see
(2) to
(3) working
(4) to do my homework / playing
(5) living
(6) to eat

❹ Activity for Accuracy

Activity 2 : It's not quite right …

- I enjoy to perform on stage.(X) → I enjoy performing on stage.(O)
- I hope learning Spanish and have recently started attending an evening course.(X) → I hope to learn Spanish and have recently started attending an evening course.(O)
- I have decided looking for a job that will help me~(X). → I have decided to look for a job that will help me~(O).

❾ TOEIC To부정사, 동명사

01. b, 02. c, 03. c, 04. b, 05. a

UNIT 08 It is helpful to get rest

❶ Introduction

(Example Answers)

I had a cold last week. So, I took a rest at home and saw a doctor.

❷ Grammar Focus

A. Complete the conversation with can, can't, should, or shouldn't

Should / should / shouldn't / can / can / can't / should

B. Request & Suggestions

(possible answers)
(Location : At work) suggest / try
(Location : At a drugstore) May / Could / Could / try

UNIT 09 What would you like?

❸ Basic Grammar

So, too, neither, either

A. Write responses to show agreement with these statements.

(1) Neither am I., (2) So can I., (3) So do I.
(4) Neither can I., (5) I'm not either., (6) I can't either.
(7) So do I., (8) I do, too., (9) Neither do I., (10) I do, too.

Modal verbs would and will for requests

C. Complete this conversation.

would / 'll(will) / Would / 'd(would) / would / 'll(will) / like

❹ Grammar Focus

Conversation 2

Grammar : Embedded Questions

B.

(1) what time the movie starts
(2) Mia is coming to the party
(3) when summer vacation begins
(4) how I should solve it
(5) we needed an extra day

❺ Conversation

B. Comprehension Check Exercise

(1) Marie could save $3 by ordering the value meal.
(2) She had her meal in the restaurant. (She dined in the burger.)
(3) She asked the cashier for burgers with fried onion and some drinks.

UNIT 10 What a big world!

❷ Reading & Basic Grammar

Reading 1

higher than / much

Grammar : Comparative and Superlative Adjectives

B.

(1) taller, (2) more exciting, (3) smaller, (4) shorter

C.

(1) the tallest, (2) worst, (3) most friendly, (4) hottest

❸ Grammar Focus

A.

- sunny - sunnier
- hot - hotter
- healthy - healthier
- famous - more famous
- fat - flatter
- expensive - more expensive
- dirty - dirtier
- crowded - more crowded
- interesting - more interesting
- easy - easier
- good - better
- beautiful - more beautiful

B.

(1) smaller, (2) higher, (3) more crowded, (4) bigger
(5) easier, (6) worse, (7) more interesting,
(8) more important, (9) better, (10) happier

C.

(1) the best, (2) the most beautiful, (3) the most famous
(4) the most effective, (5) the best, (6) the worst
(7) the most exciting, (8) the most embarrassing

❻ TOEIC LC 의문사 의문문

CHECK-UP

(1) 고장이 났다, (2) 출퇴근하다, (3) 교차로, (4) 내려주다
(5) ~로 향해 가는, (6) 직항편

❼ TOEIC RC 비교급, 원급비교, 최상급

비교급, 원급비교

(01) a, (02) b, (03) b, (04) b, (05) b, (06) a

최상급

(01) b, (02) b, (03) b, (04) b, (05) a, (06) d

UNIT 11 What are you doing later?

❷ Conversation

Conversation 2

(1) d. aunt and uncle
(2) c. Rome
(3) b. plane
(4) a. five days

❹ Conversation & Basic Grammar

Grammar : Be going to & Will

B.

(1) is going to visit
(2) will call
(3) are going to take / will not be
(4) will not take
(5) will have
(6) am going to graduate

❺ Exercise -one morning with Jack

Question 1. B
Question 2. C
Question 3. A
Question 4. B
Question 5. C

❼ Activity -Hit the Road

(Linda's diary notes)

I'm flying to Tokyo tomorrow. My uncle is about to arrive to lend me his Japanese phrasebook. My plane leaves at 6am. I'm going to stay with a Japanese family for three weeks. Then I'm working in an orphanage in Thailand. I will learn Spanish in Chile. I've already booked a one-month Spanish language course in Santiago.

UNIT 12 Polite and diplomatic language

❷ Exercise

01. I'd like a hamburger. (or, I'll have a hamburger, please.)
02. Could you send me the report?
03. Could you give me a minute? (or, Sorry, I'm a bit busy right now.)
04. Let me know when you're available.
05. /
06. I'm not so sure that's a good idea. (or, I have a few concerns.)
07. I'm not quite satisfied with this work. (or, to be honest, this needs some improvement.)
08. I'm not too fond of the colors in this design. (or, I'd prefer to use different colors in this design.)
09. The lady who is wearing white blouse is not feeling comfortable due to lack of personal space. I would try to offer another seat if there are any empty seats available.

❸ Grammar Focus -Relative Pronouns

Activity 1

(01) a, (02) h, (03) g, (04) l, (05) k, (06) f, (07) b,
(08) d, (09) c, (10) e

Activity 2

01. I met a man who can speak English very well.
02. Jack who is my brother is playing soccer there.
03. I have a friend who knows a lot of celebrities.
04. I like a person who can share the same hobby with me.
05. I know someone who can help you.
06. This is the book that I've wanted to buy.
07. The hotel where we stayed was the Silla Hotel.
08. I visited a beautiful city which was in France.
09. I met a person who works for a famous IT company in San Francisco.
10. I met him in Singapore which is known as a multicultural country.
11. It is Singapore where I met the client last month.
12. I met a man whose name is 유재석.

❺ Practice More

A.

01. who, 02. where, 03. which, 04. who, 05. where,
06. when, 07. where, 08. which

B.

01. The last time I saw my best friend who is from Australia was at a festival.
02. Have you watched that film that I recommended to you last month yet?
03. I've never met that woman (who) my cousin is talking to.
04. I want to buy that handbag which has grey buttons.
05. I'll never forget that moment when I met my boyfriend.
06. This is the playground where we used to play every day as children.
07. That's the window that was broken last week.

저자약력

▪ 백선숙

세종대학교 호텔관광경영학박사
숙명여자대학교 TESOL 국제영어교사
경복대학교 항공서비스과 겸임교수
숭의여자대학교 IT소프트웨어융합과 외래교수
Singapore Airlines 객실승무원

▪ 강희준

현) 인하공업전문대학 관광경영학과 교수
한국항공대학교 경영학박사(항공경영전공)
China Airlines 서울여객지점 여객영업마케팅부 근무
항공경영학회, 한국관광진흥학회, 한국관광산업학회 이사

Global English
취업성공을 위한 글로벌 영어

발행일 I 2023년 3월 10일 발행

발행인 I 모흥숙
발행처 I 도서출판 새로미

저 자 I 백선숙 · 강희준

주 소 I 서울 용산구 한강대로 104라길 3
전 화 I 02) 523-5903~4
팩 스 I 02) 775-3246

E-mail I seromi@seromi.kr
Homepage I www.seromi.kr

ISBN I 978-89-6476-814-3 93740
정 가 I 20,000원
